CW01672985

for Sienna

Willow

with best wishes,

Kate

August 2003

"The end of May is a dreaded time. You get the full moon end of May and you can get a frost, we haven't had one for a year or two. What we normally do about the end of May - we've usually got withies anything from six inches, well a few inches high, up to a foot high - we pray for rain, pray for cloudy overcast miserable windy weather, 'cos you won't get a frost then obviously. If you get nice settled dry weather, sleepless nights then I'm afraid for a while, 'til the moon's over. End of May, make you or break you May will, traditionally known."

BRIAN LOCK
willow grower
Kingsbury Episcopi

Published by Furlong Fields Publishing
in association with The Brewhouse, Taunton
Paintings and drawings by Kate Lynch ©
Compiled by Kate Lynch
Designed by Catherine Phelps epicdg@teleline.es
Reproduction by Lucam
Printed by Torreangulo
2003, ISBN No. 0-9544394-0-6
D.L.: M-5.520-2003

Front cover:
Brian Lock in the pit with willows for stripping as white, oil on paper
Inside front cover:
Pete Nicholas bordering down, willow charcoal on paper

Willow

KATE LYNCH

Paintings and drawings
with Somerset voices

FOREWORD BY DAVID BELLAMY

CONTENTS

FOREWORD
WILLOW WANDS

DAVID BELLAMY Itinerant Botanist

'Bordering down', 'growing on for whites', 'moor out', 'randing and waling', 'reaps and willy's', 'slewing a hurdle', 'spiling', 'straightforward bottoms', 'stripped withies', 'three rod wale' and 'upsetting'. Local words of wisdom whisper from a past now almost lost in the mists that rise up from the sodden skirts of Avalon. One can only guess how many words and phrases are disappearing, as more and more dialects go to the wall of extinction. The good news is that some of these Somerset expressions live on, as this wonderful book amply demonstrates.

Willows came naturally to Somerset, taming the flood waters around the meanders of the rivers Parrett, Tone, Axe, Cary and Yeo, long before people learned the common sense of it all and fastened a bundle of withies with the rose knot, marking their pride in a job well done. A hallmark of sustainable practice if ever there was one. And as the willows contained the floods, the pulses of the waters were calmed enough for oxygen to come in short supply. This stifled the pace of decay and organic peat could begin to form, filling the hollows, creating one of the rarest, and most beautiful, of Mother Nature's living mosaics. The hard-worked mix of cut-away, levels, sedge moor, rhynes and rivers is still a wet, watery wonderland in which otters, kingfishers and a host of now-rare wildlife and wildflowers, can mind their own business, along with the willow growers, cutters, boilers, strippers, basketmakers, hurdlers, weavers, fishers, artists and artisans celebrated in this book.

Even in the case of willow wands, the Second World War was the mother of reinvention. Local expertise was needed on the Home Front and did its level best to supply baskets of all shapes and sizes, pliant, yet strong enough, to carry explosives, and to house that forgotten flying corps, the pigeons, silent heroes who carried messages far and wide. With the end of the war, plastics and electronics threatened willow growing and basket-making, but they still live on, organic to the roots.

Willow bark is an organic febrifuge that gave the world the 'greenprint' of Aspirin, used to this day to ward off headaches and to thin the blood. In my youth, biscuits made of willow charcoal still found favour in the treatment of flatulence and dysentery, while, as Kate Lynch's work proves, a stick of artist's charcoal in the right hands produces real life pictures as organic as the scenes they depict.

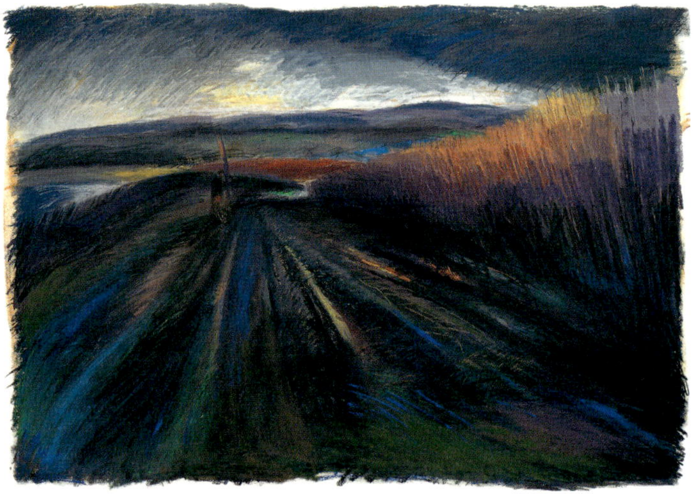

Today, with global warming bringing torrential rain and floods, the art of spiling - weaving living willow to protect river banks - and the crafting of enormous willow mats to slow coastal erosion, is reawakening the industry once again. What is more, willow sculptures are becoming a vibrant living heritage in playgrounds, hospitals and hospices, and even top hotels. Real, cool living, green space in which the stress of modern living can suffuse away thanks to the homeopathy of waving willow wands.

This collection of atmospheric paintings and drawings by Kate Lynch, with their Somerset voices, is a tribute to the people who cultivate the willow and craft its wood, and it is also a beacon for future generations. I am often asked what can I do to help save the living world? Why not buy a willow basket and always take it with you to the shops? Of course you could choose a woodland burial in a willow coffin and so become a tree.

Withy Harvest, Stan Moor

"Good weather then, warm like, lovely warm nights then they grow, they grow around about an inch a day."

STAN DERHAM
willow grower
Knapp, North Curry

WITHY HARVEST

"Well they grow til the end of August and then in September they stouten. You can start cutting towards the end of October, the leaf begins to drop. When you start in the beginning of the season you get the backache but only for the first two or three days. You're much better off when you're stooped down than you are if you're on a half stoop, like if you were hoeing mangles, that would be more likely to give you the backache than what cutting withies would"

REG HECTOR
willow grower
North Curry

Reg Hector and Mark Pipe cutting out, Wick Moor

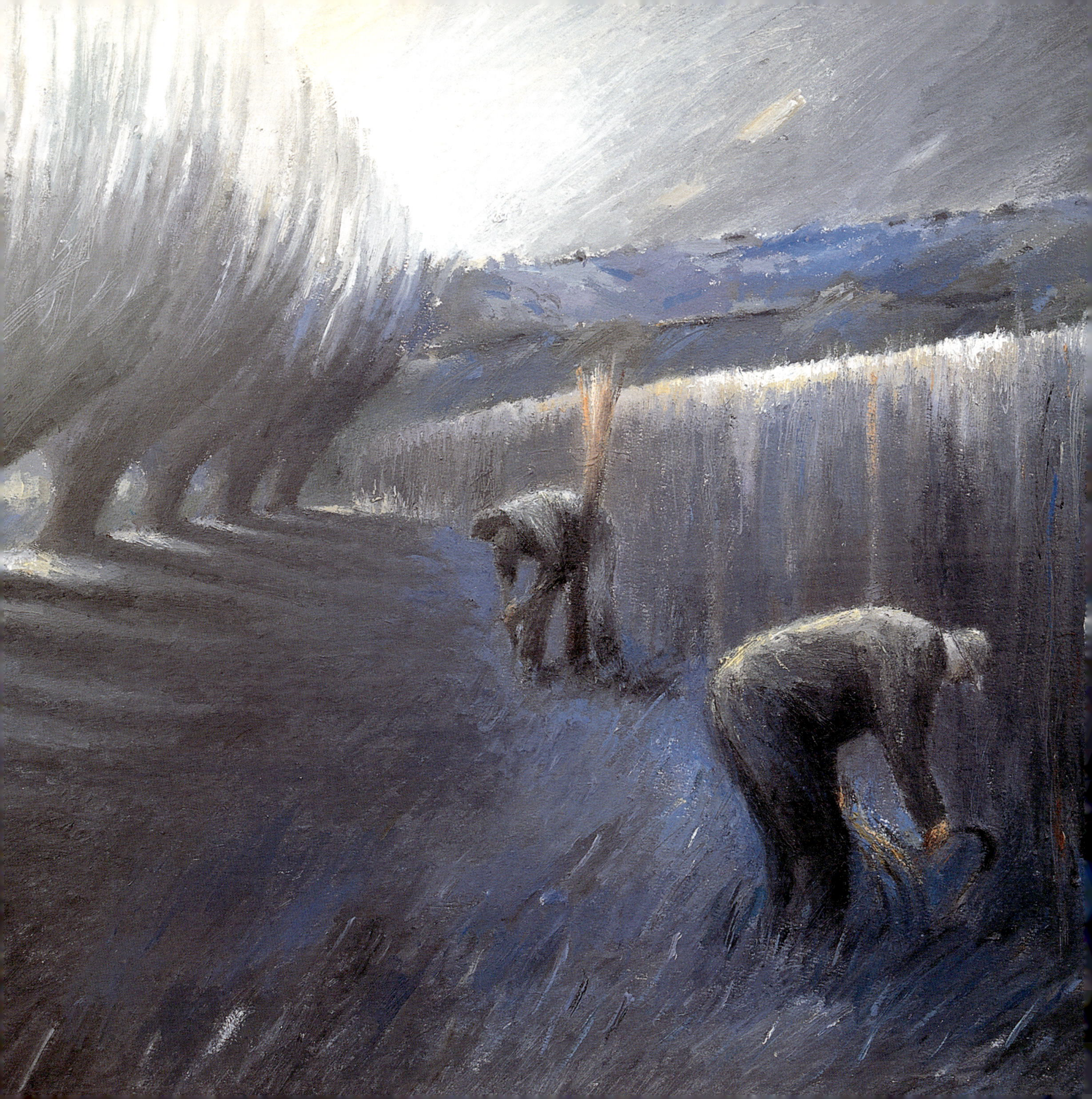

"Around here you've got clay soil. Willows like clay. You can have twenty, I suppose, in a good-producing bed, perhaps twenty willows on a stump. If you get around two hundred or two hundred and fifty bundles per acre you've got a good crop. We start cutting when all the leaf's off and it's dormant, the sap's gone down in the willow. We cut all through the winter, right out to the end of April. You just go out the droves to the willow beds, go out in the morning, bit of a messy job. No matter what we cut in one day we try to bring home, because you never know when the water's coming in. We've had, in the last few years, a lot more rain than was normal, and moors that hadn't flooded, not for sixty years, had water in for about three years running. There's only one moor, Stan Moor, that's really free of water now. It was in 1929 the big flood. What they tell me was, we had a lot of rain, started raining August time, I think, and went on out 'til Christmas and past, and then we had a bit of snow, and what they say is, the tide flowed twice, came up, and the wind blew it up, and the moor bank broke and flooded all of Stan Moor."

GEORGE DAVID
Willow grower
Burrowbridge

Withy harvest, Hills Bed, Stan Moor

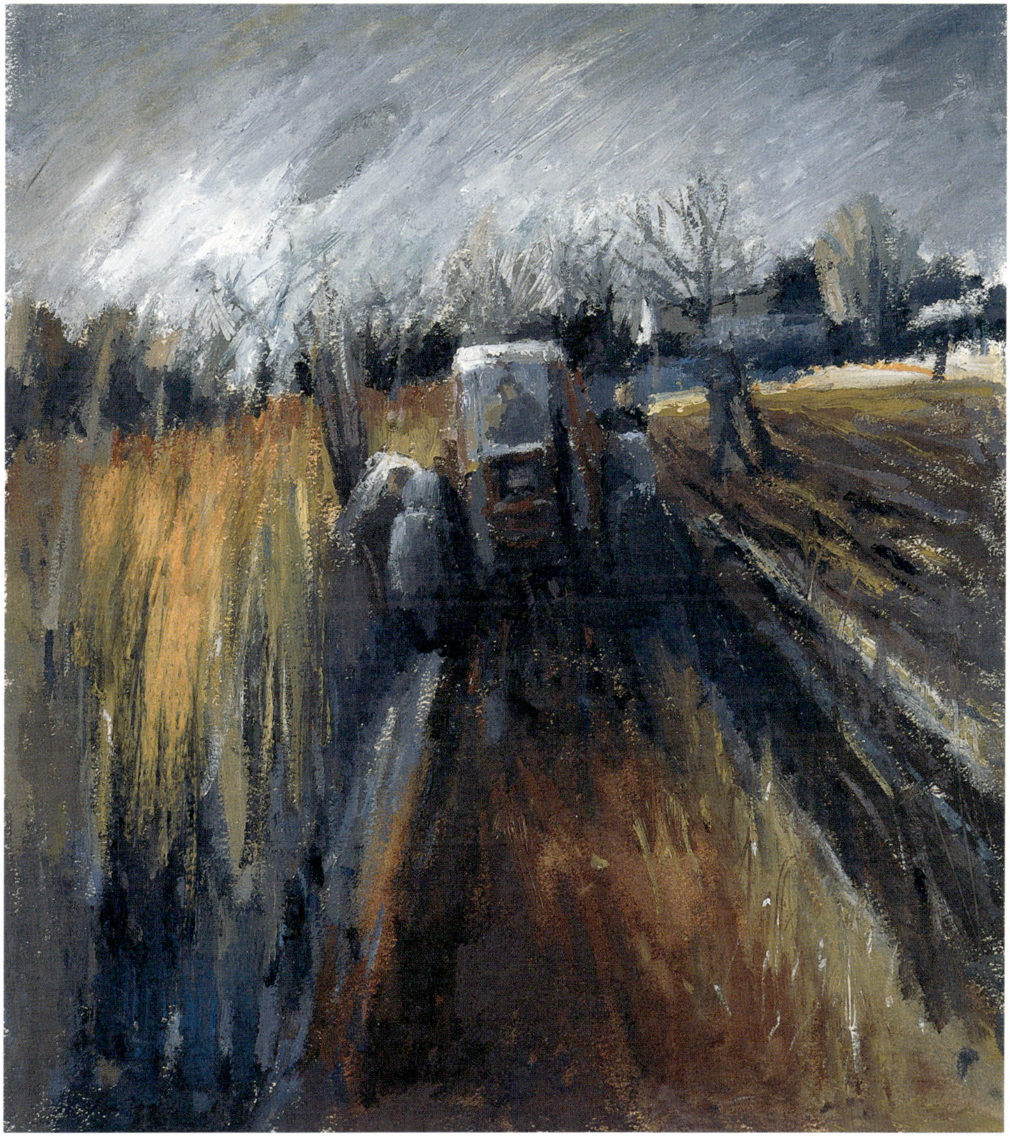

"You're down on the moors in the worst weather you've got through the winter, and you've just got to keep going all day, stop for a quick smoke now and then, and your dinner, apart from that you've got to keep going."

MARK PIPE

Mark Pipe cutting out, Wick Moor

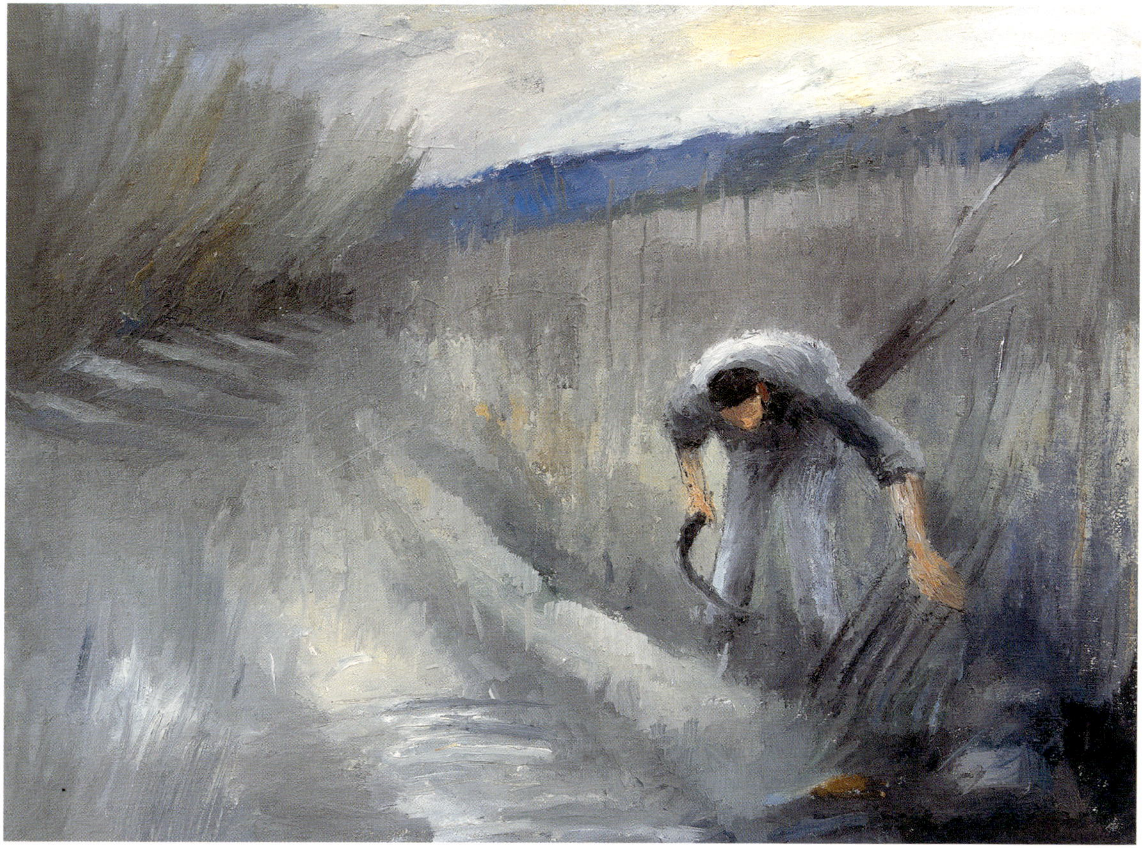

"I was cutting when I left school, fourteen. We had an old people's party up here last Saturday afternoon and there's a chap Eddy Male, he was there, and we were talking about the old days because he's eighty nearly and he was down West Moor. He said 'I can remember when you came down, the first day, you cut ten bundles.' Fourteen year old. 'Cos Father was cutting about forty odd! But you wouldn't let fourteen year olds now, they think they've just started school! We used to cut our feet and hands and all sorts. We used to always start cutting about the 17th November and, well, most of the leaves were off, that was Father's birthday, he'd have his birthday then we'd start! We've been down there wet through in the winters. I've been down there today cutting by hand for a customer. I counted thirty swans in a field there next to me, just over the drain there, thirty swans this morning."

LESLIE MALE
willow grower
Stembridge

Leslie Male cutting, Collins Bed, West Moor

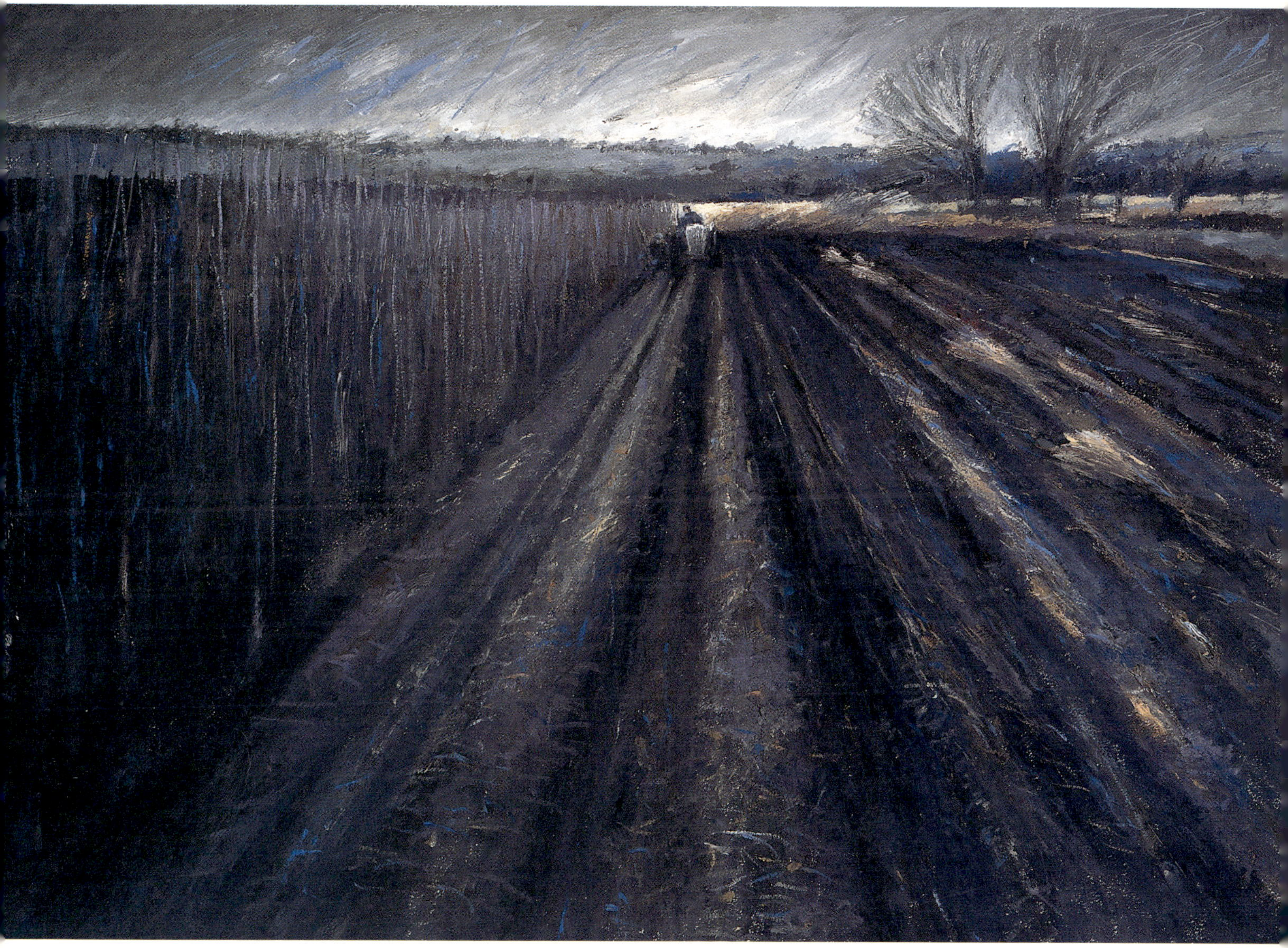

"The first one was at Woodhill, Stoke St. Gregory at the Rose and Crown, that one was in October, the next one was at Langport at the Railway Arms, the next one was at North Curry, which was the biggest sale, at the Bird in Hand, and that was always beginning of November. In those days I used to go cutting withies so we always went to the sales because the merchants who bought the withies at the sales used to try to get their cutters, and the auctioneers, as an incentive to the buyers, they gave tickets according to the amount of willows you bought. Of course, if you bought a large amount of willows you got a large amount of vouchers and they came round to the cutters and offered vouchers for drinks to try to get them one over the eight if they could, to try to persuade them to cut their withies instead of the next man's! I don't ever remember any rowdiness going on, it was a jolly occasion always."

REG HECTOR
willow grower
North Curry

Reg Hector cutting out, Wick Moor

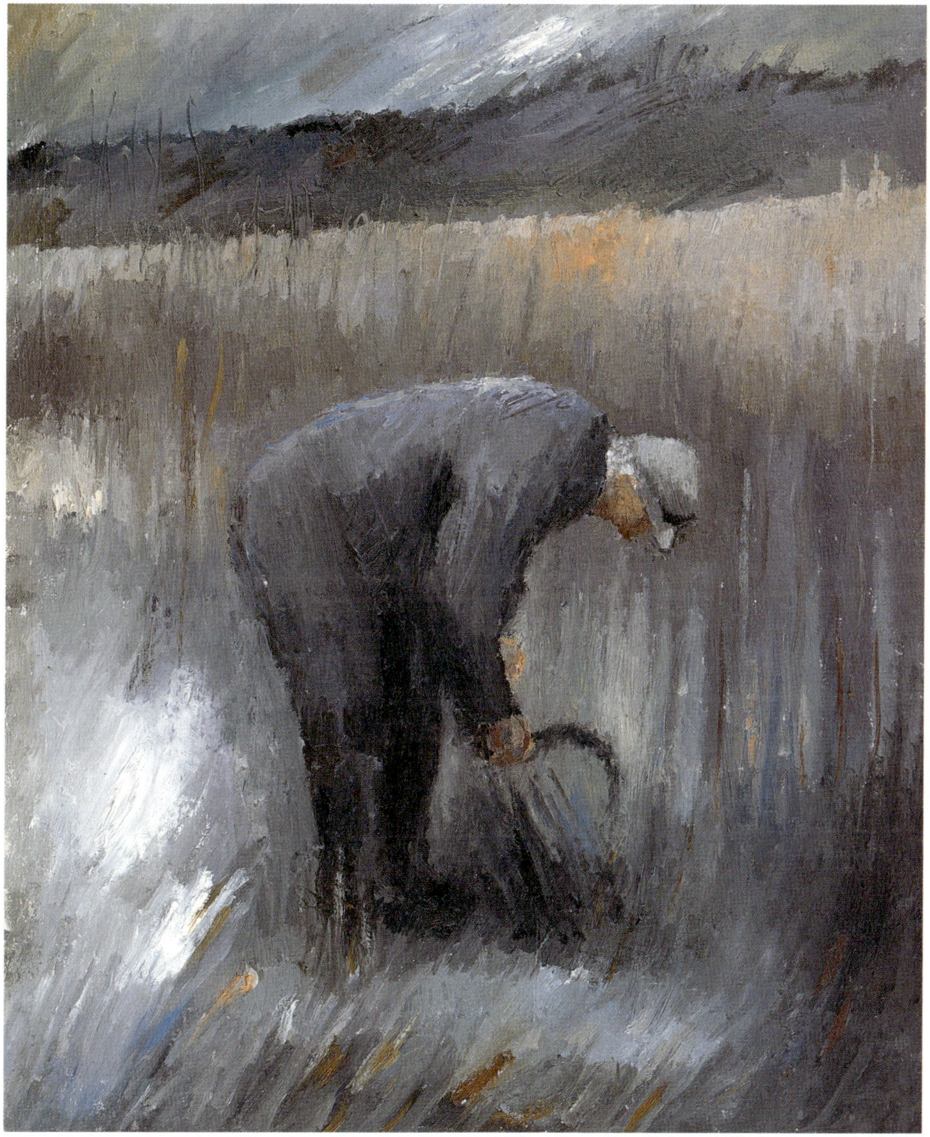

"If there's a lot of leaf you mustn't stack 'em, they've got to be stood upright, because we find they will heat and once they start heating with their leaf on it spoils the willow and they don't keep the same. At the moment I'm sorting and then picking them all over. Once they come off the Levels they're brought home, we pick out all the rough willow and just put the best of the willow for basketmaking. Rough willow, that is what the basketmaker wouldn't want. They can't make a nice basket with the rough scraggy willow".

CLIFFORD HEMBROW
North Curry

Clifford Hembrow sorting withies, North Curry

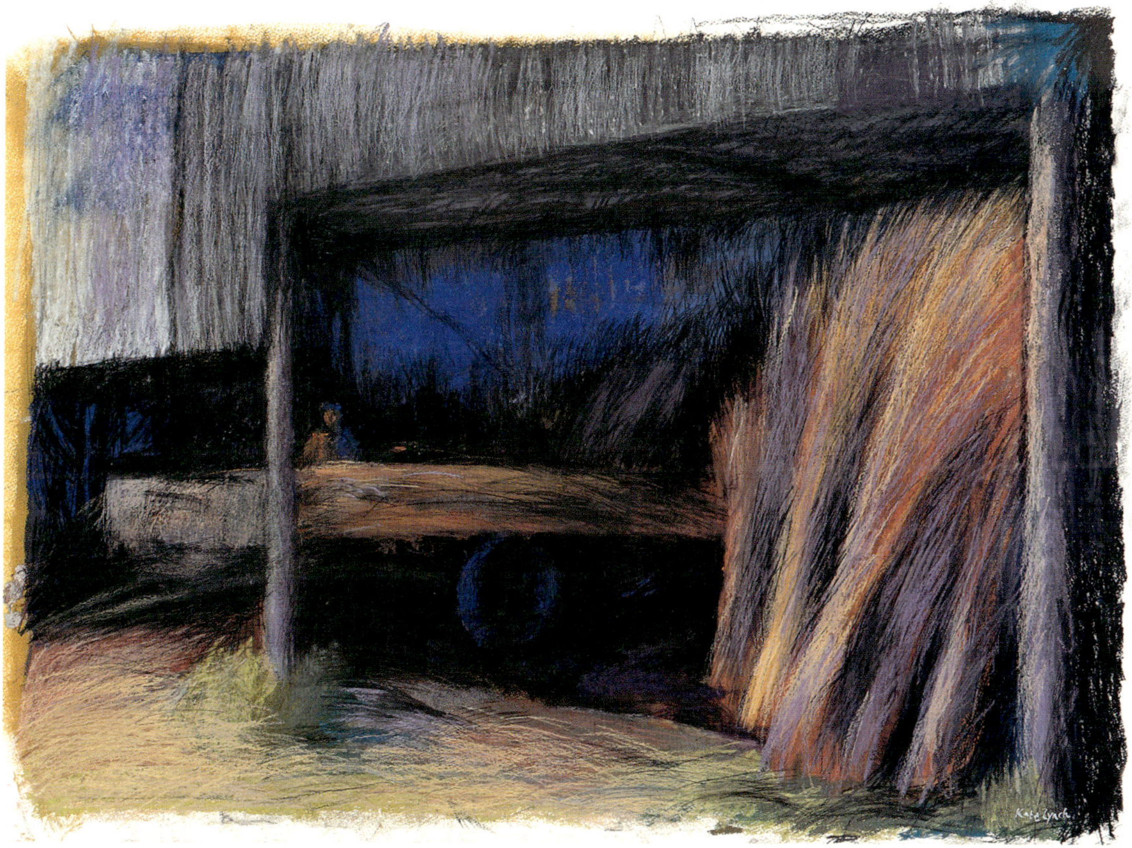
Kate Lynch

WHITENING, BOILING AND STRIPPING

"From Christmas you're busy, boiling for buff and you've got people wanting brown, last year's withies, and the moors might flood, so you just cut what you can and put a few in the pit each week for the white. That keeps them artificially alive, then in the spring they start to sprout, what we call 'moor out' and leaf out and then you can strip them white, when the sap's in them. Whites are dearer because you've got to watch them all the time, top the water up, look after them, and you don't do so many. Then you need a sunny, windy day to strip them, they have to be dried quickly to keep the colour, too much moisture for too long after they're stripped and it stains the willow and they're not the bright white. You can't strip them much after three in the afternoon and be sure of putting them away that day."

STEPHEN PEARCE
willow grower
Stoke St. Gregory

Brian Lock in the pit with withies for stripping as white

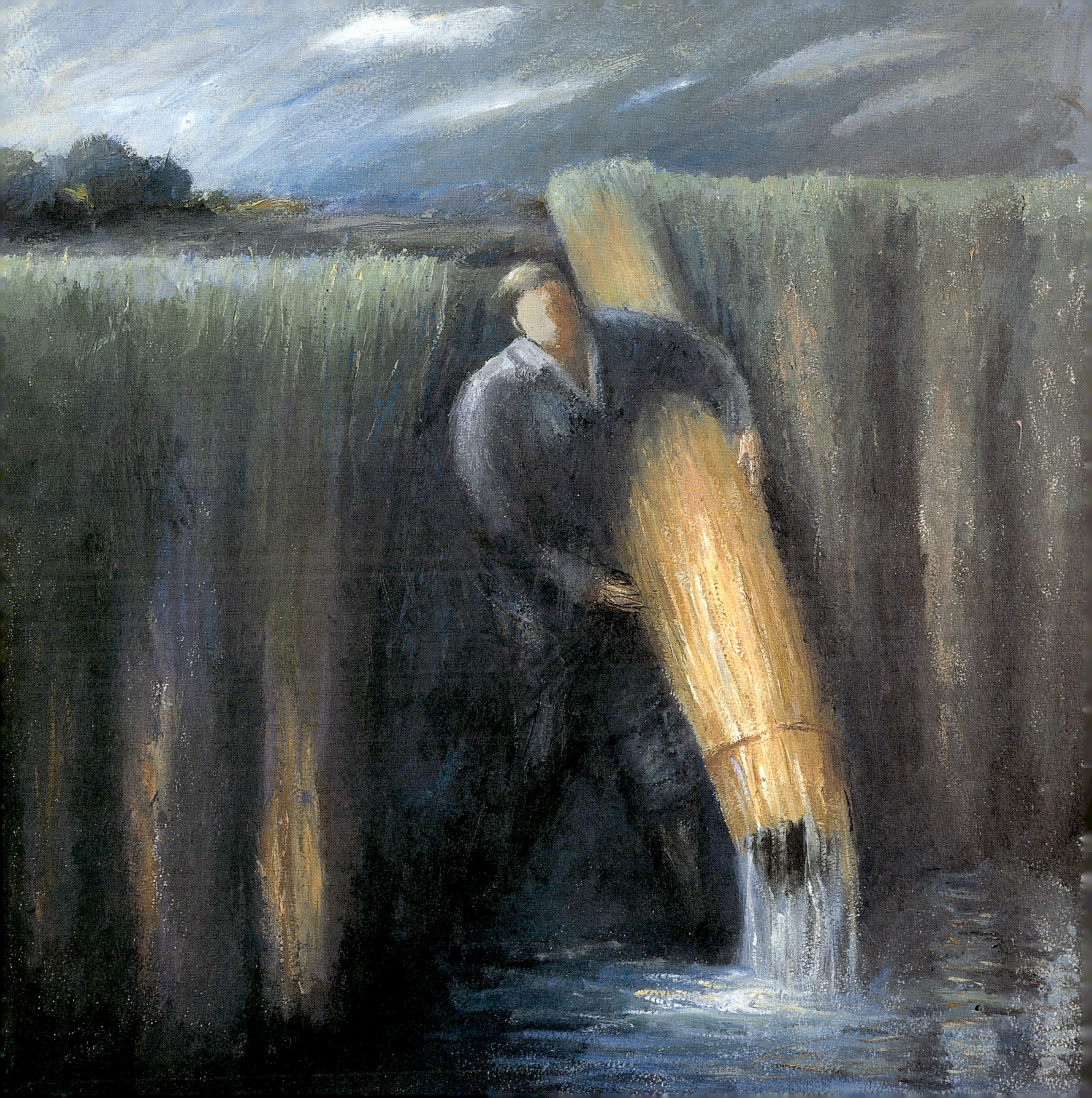

"We usually cut those at Christmas or just after Christmas, freshly cut, and we sort them straight-away. Then we stack them in the pits. Then they're left there 'til May, and then we strip them. We just strip the bark straight off them green and they're pure white then, and then we just stand them to dry the same as we do the buff, but they don't take very long to dry. You know if you get a nice day, which you do at that time of year, you can dry them easily in a day, strip them in the mornings and bring them in in the evenings".

BRIAN WHITE
willow grower
Kingsbury Episcopi

The Whitening Season

Brian Lock and Brian White drying stripped whites

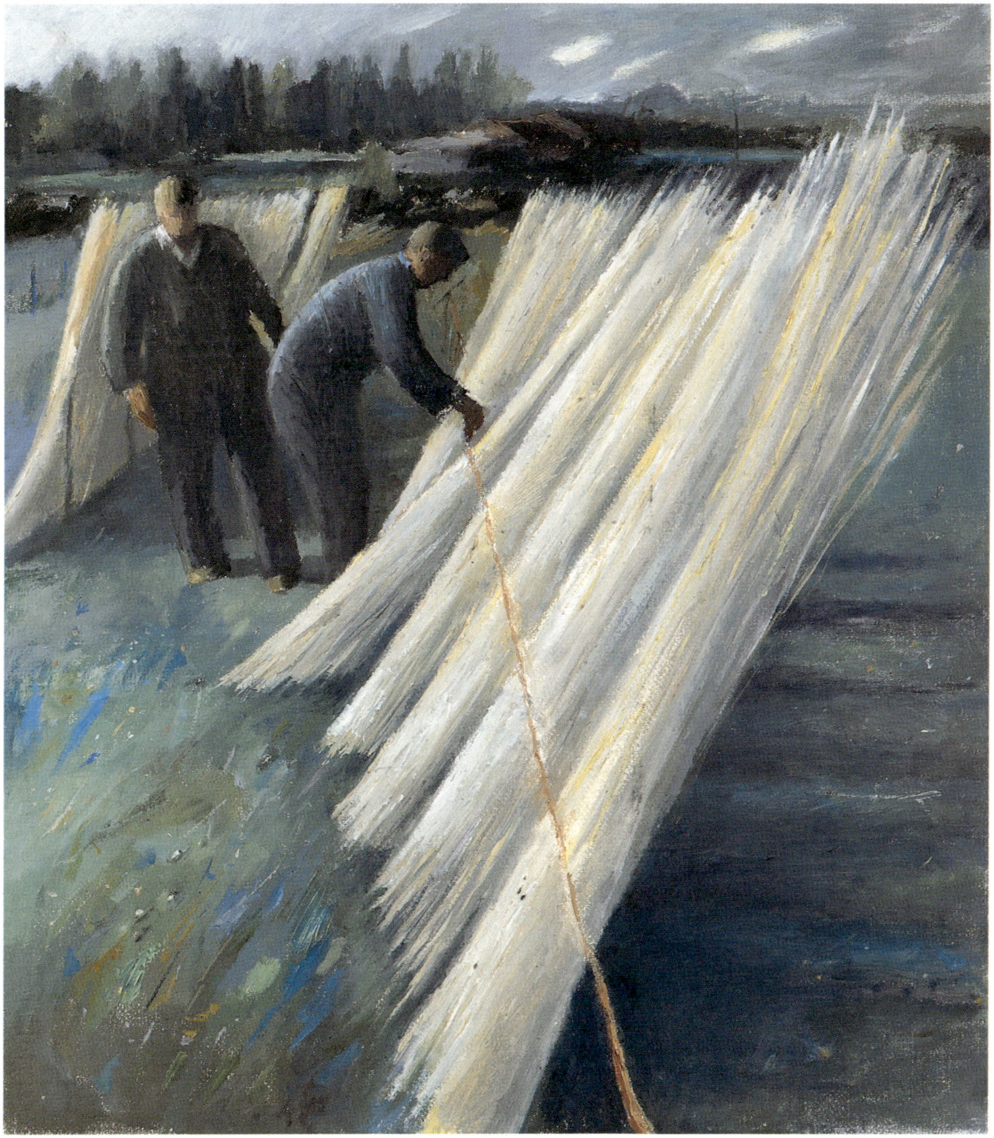

"There's one most important thing: it is for the green willow, you must have the water boiling, boiling really hard, hot water to put the green willow in and boil 'em from then on, otherwise they won't strip. If you put them in cold water you're wasting your time, but the harvest willow, you can put them in cold water and boil them from there and they'll strip alright. That's the most important thing about it. The rest is just keeping a good fire under the boiler and watching it doesn't boil over and adding a drop of water in there, keep the water up. If you haven't got the water up over the willows they'll burn and you won't strip 'em. It's about about a twelve hour process, from about eight in the morning to eight at night."

GEORGE DAVID
willow grower
Burrowbridge

George David boiling withies for stripping as buff

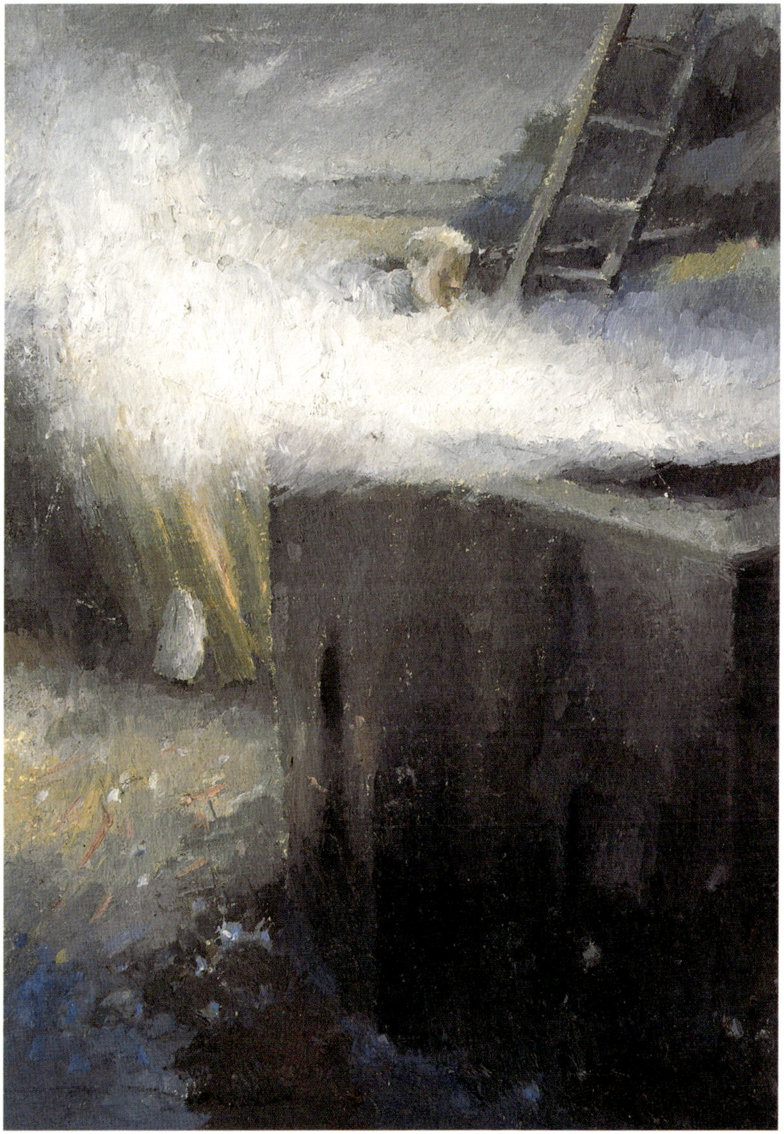

"The war came on and we had three machines going five days a week and boiling every day for five days a week and the boiler would hold about a hundred and sixty half bundles, because if you had them in bundles you would have a job to move them around, carry them, especially with women working on it. I didn't have to go in the Forces because our willows were more important than going in the Army or growing corn. The Air Ministry was one of our main customers. They wanted for us to grow more willow because they wanted all these baskets. Every aeroplane and every ship used to carry pigeons, so they all wanted pigeon baskets and then you had your big baskets to drop supplies to the troops. They'd go out of shape, but they wouldn't break."

MAURICE DERHAM
retired willow grower
Knapp, North Curry

Chris Derham boiling withies for stripping as buff

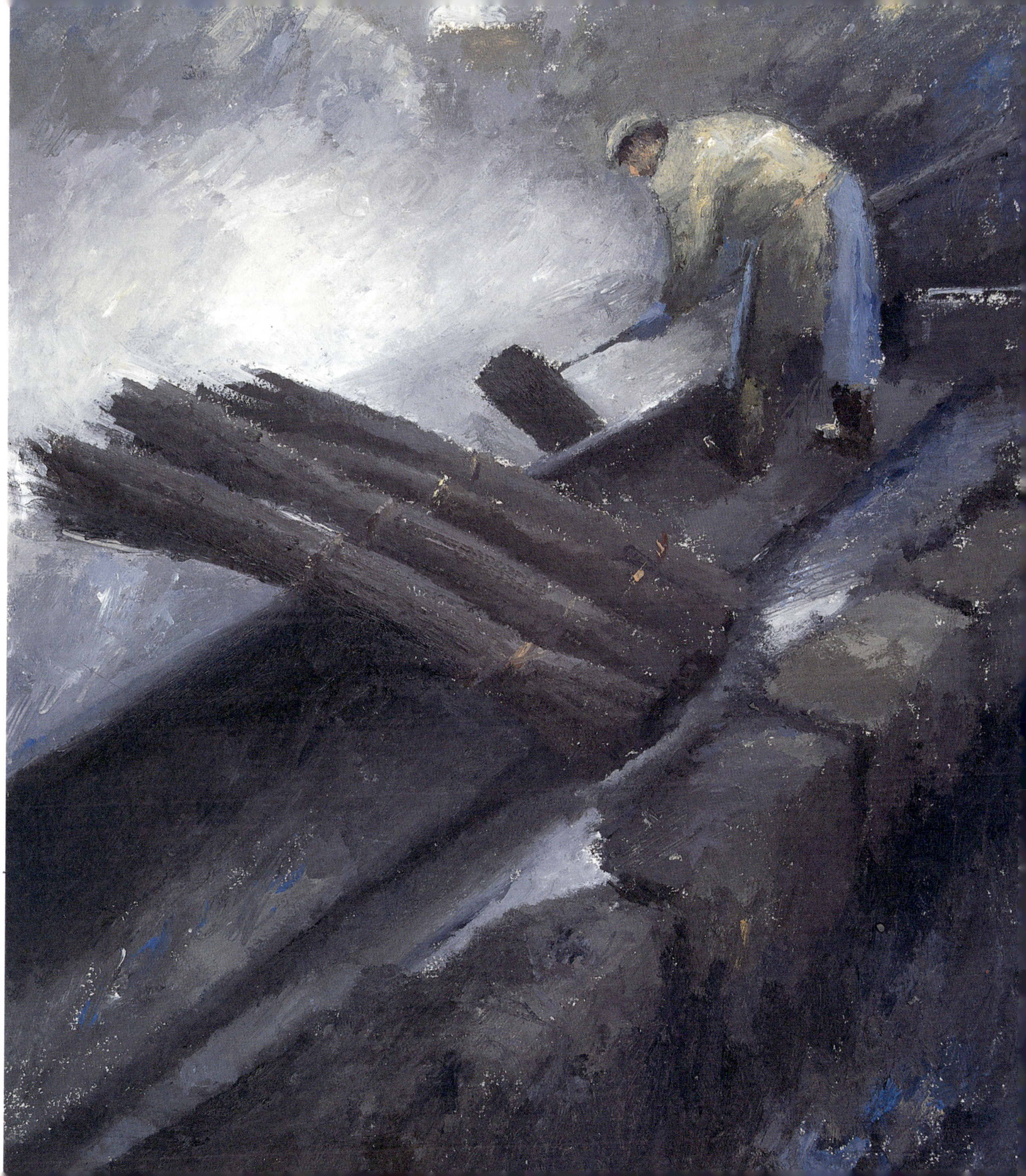

"We've got an apron, plastic apron, that we tie on, because of the tannin out of the willow. I expect you've seen. I use gloves in the winter, we use gloves most of the time. In the summer, when it's a bit hot we don't use them, but your hands, they get really black with the stain out of the willow and it just won't come off whatever you do, it's got to wear off gradually. Brian's father used to do it all the time, stripping willow, and his hands were jet black, absolutely black, and he used to go to the football matches in the town and the people did not know what willows were ten miles away from here and they wouldn't understand why his hands were so black."

BRIAN WHITE
willow grower
Kingsbury Episcopi
(speaking of his father-in-law, Herbert Lock)

Chris Derham stripping boiled withies for buff

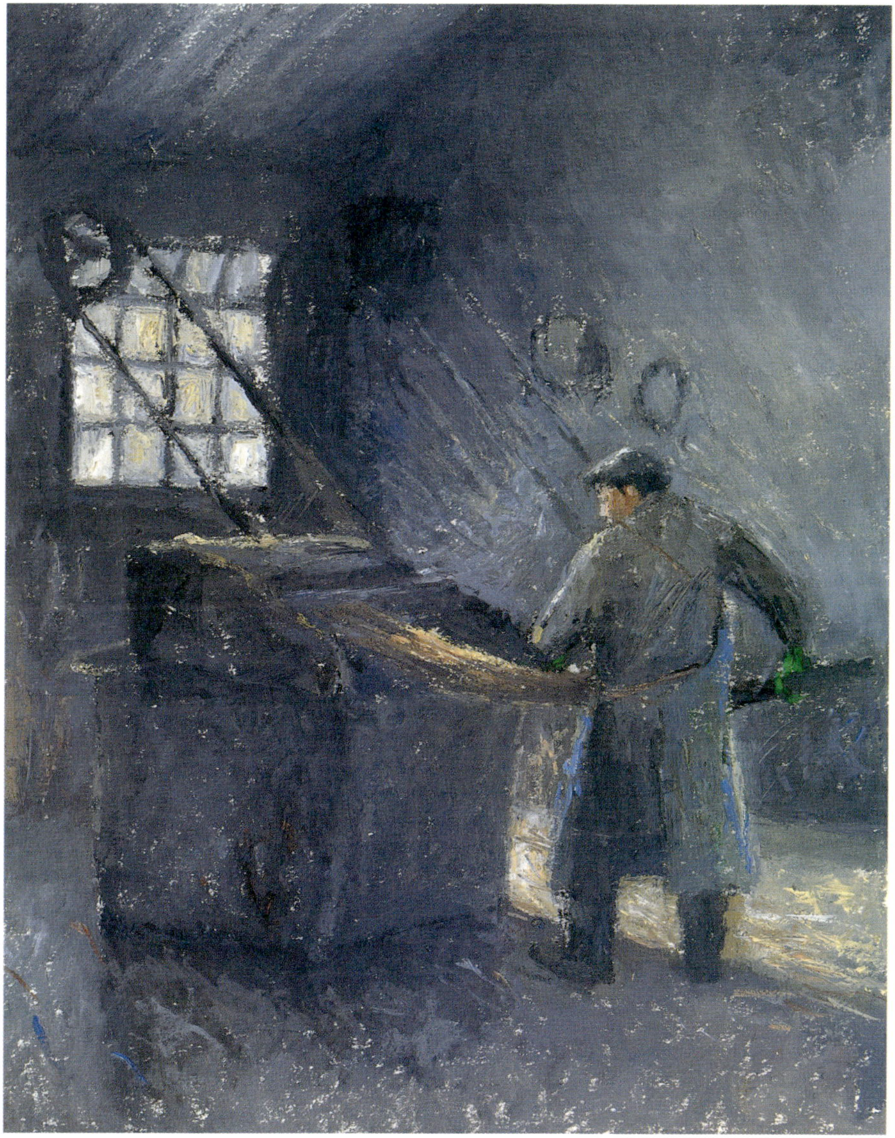

"We used to have twenty people working here, we had a lot of acres of willows. There's only my nephew and I doing it now. I can go back to when a bundle of buck willows was about fifteen and sixpence where now they be over twenty quid. I came up here one night after all the workers were gone when I was about twelve year old and I thought to myself 'I'm going to tie a bundle of willows'. So I made my two binds and I tied the bundle of withies, put 'em back in the stack where all the rest were put, what the men had tied that day, and nobody ever noticed that I tied a bundle of willows and from that day I kept going.

Getting the bark off is done in the stripping machines, the willow stripping is one of the hardest jobs, years ago they were done in what you call the hand-brakes, one at a time, but now it's done in big handfuls. We used to take them round to all the cottages and at one time all the women used to have a brake in their garden and they used to do so many wads a day and we used to go out and get them back in the night and then in the next morning take out a few more. They used to earn aroundabout two shillings a day in those days."

STAN DERHAM
willow grower
Knapp, North Curry

Stan and Chris Derham stripping boiled withies for buff

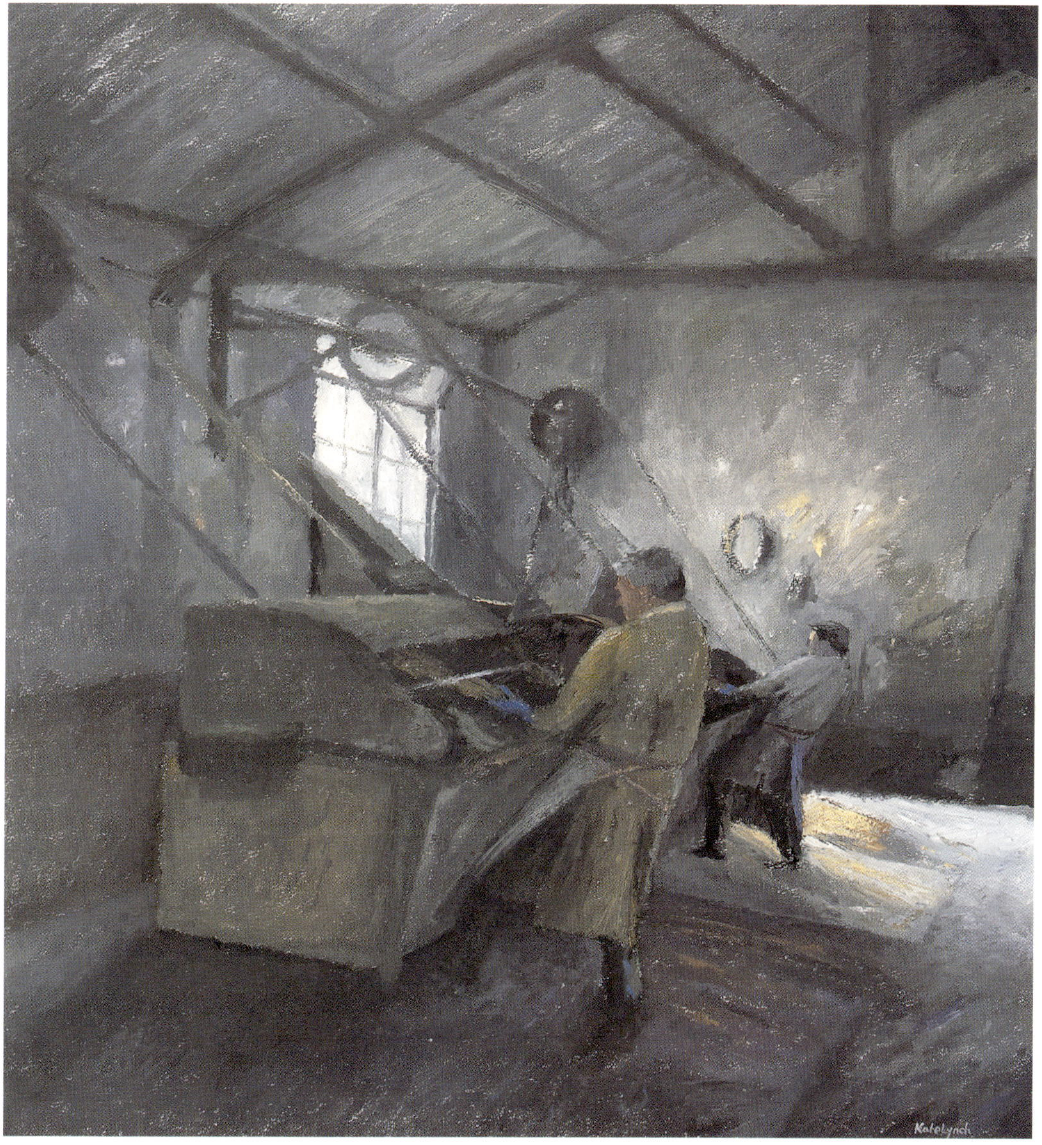
KateLynch

"It's an Eddy Storey willow stripping machine, the baker used to make them at Burrowbridge, Eddy Storey, and that's it there now, and what we do, you do the butt ends first, half way, and then turn them round and put the tops in. We've always stripped on one machine. I always do the butt ends and Dad does the tops and that's how we go around. This time of year, in October time, usually we'll strip all day 'til half past five, six o'clock. We'll have our tea and then come out after tea and spread them all then, so usually it's nearly dark before we've finished."

MICHAEL MUSGROVE
willow grower
Westonzoyland

Michael and Les Musgrove stripping and sorting

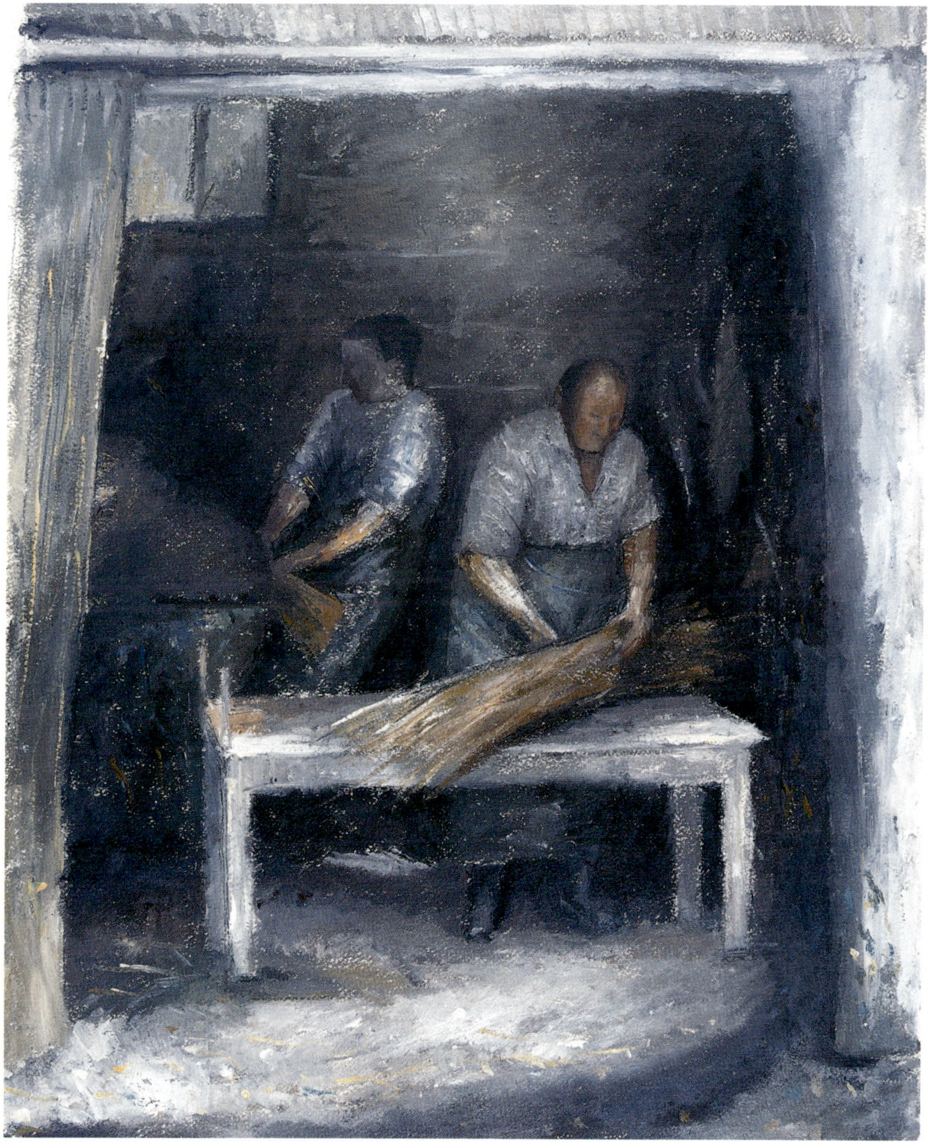

TYING

"I think as long as the sap's alive it'll keep going, but it's the labour involved, the amount of work. I've had a good life minding willows, I enjoy it. It's something you take to or you don't, but if you really like it and take to it you wouldn't really want to do anything else. I hope to survive long enough so I'm cutting by hand at eighty."

GEORGE DAVID
willow grower
Burrowbridge

George David patting the willows back

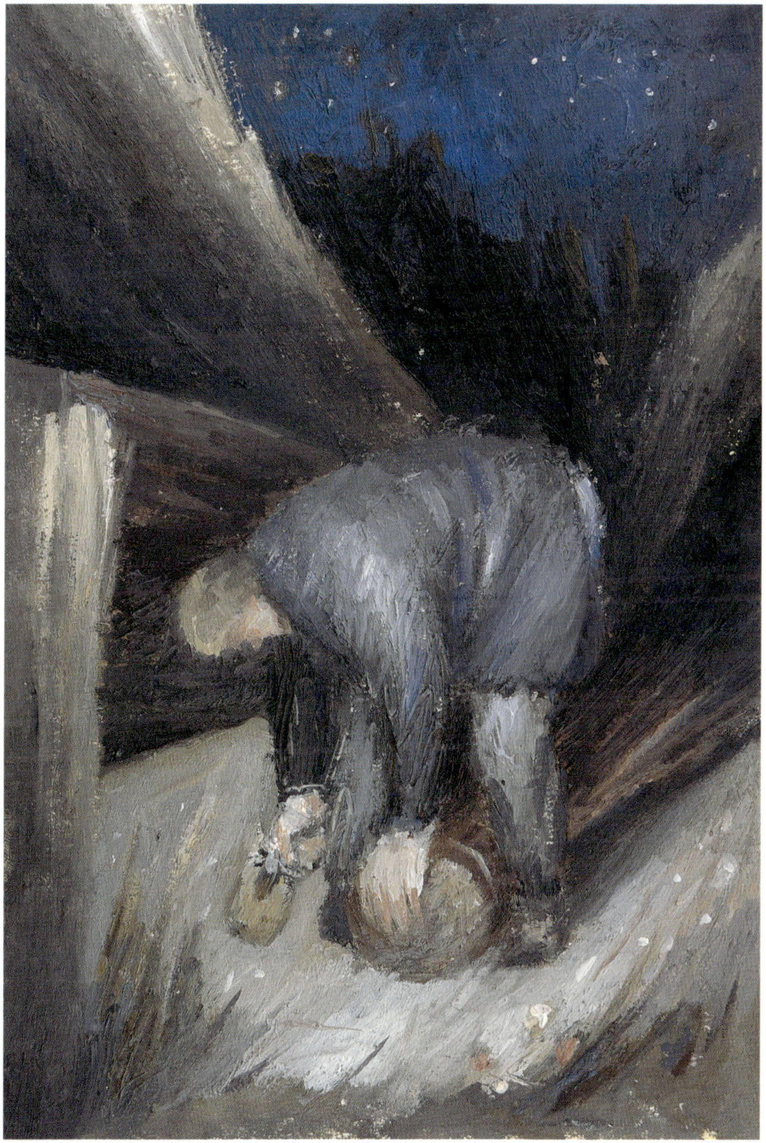

"You can usually tell whose willow you're looking at by the bond, what sort of rose, what sort of rose he puts in and how it's twisted. That all used to be done to sell the willows, that's why that all started. You know, the one who made a beautiful tie, made a nice tie, made a nice rose, that would sell your withies."

BRIAN LOCK
willow grower
Kingsbury Episcopi

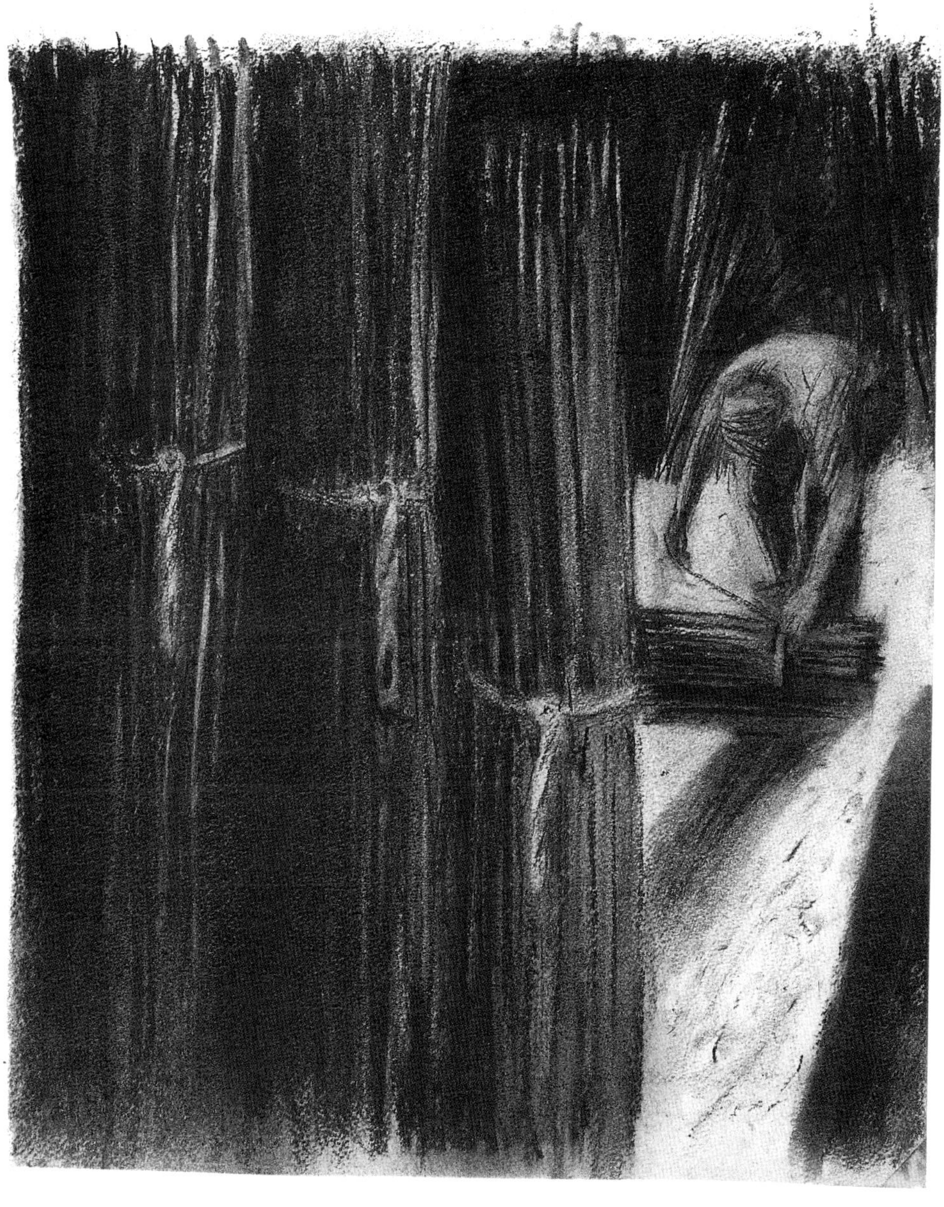

BASKETMAKING

"My two aunties were basketmakers. We had to come home from school and strip a few withies before we could go out to play. I had to do that every night when I came home from school, when the withy time was around. Stripping withies was all done by hand, we used to get paid for it, it was about two bob a bundle at the time. I was taught with Arthur Payne, Wally Hillard, Eddy Dare and Freddy Southwark, which were the top craftsmen at the time. I think it's a fantastic trade, I couldn't work in a factory or anything like that. It's so fantastic to start from a few willows and sticks and make a basket "

EDDIE BARNARD
basketmaker
Middlezoy

Eddie Barnard tapping the willows down tight

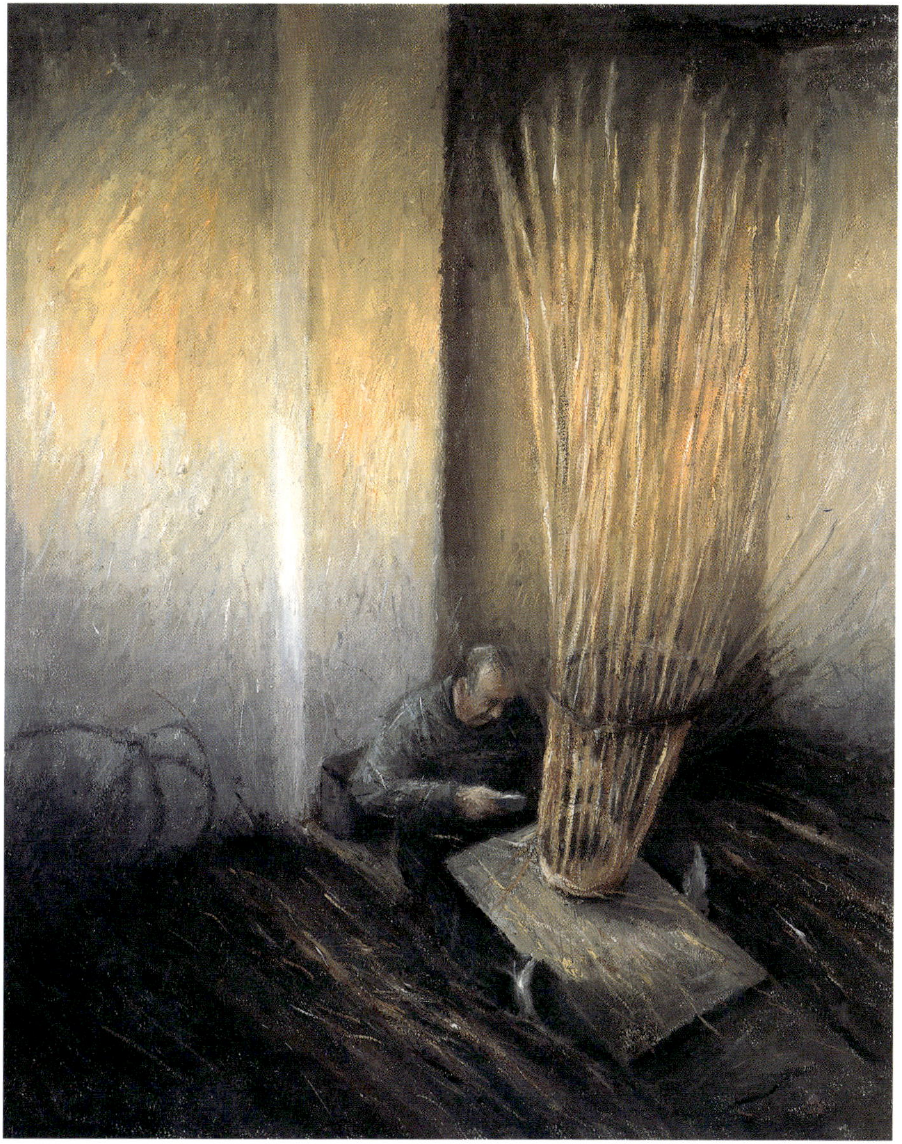

"We were about a dozen when we were called up, they came round and said they were looking for recruits to make baskets and we thought we would or we thought we might have been sent away to do some other war work. We had to make panniers for the big aircraft, it was the only way they could drop what was needed out of the sky. The young Mr. Musgrave, he was the one who was in charge of us. We'd been brought up with the withies and we had to strip them, but until this started we didn't know very much about basketmaking at all, wasn't interested I don't suppose, but when it came to a gang of us together, oh it was a fine life!"

DOREEN LOVERIDGE
retired basketmaker
Curload

Pete Nicholas bordering down

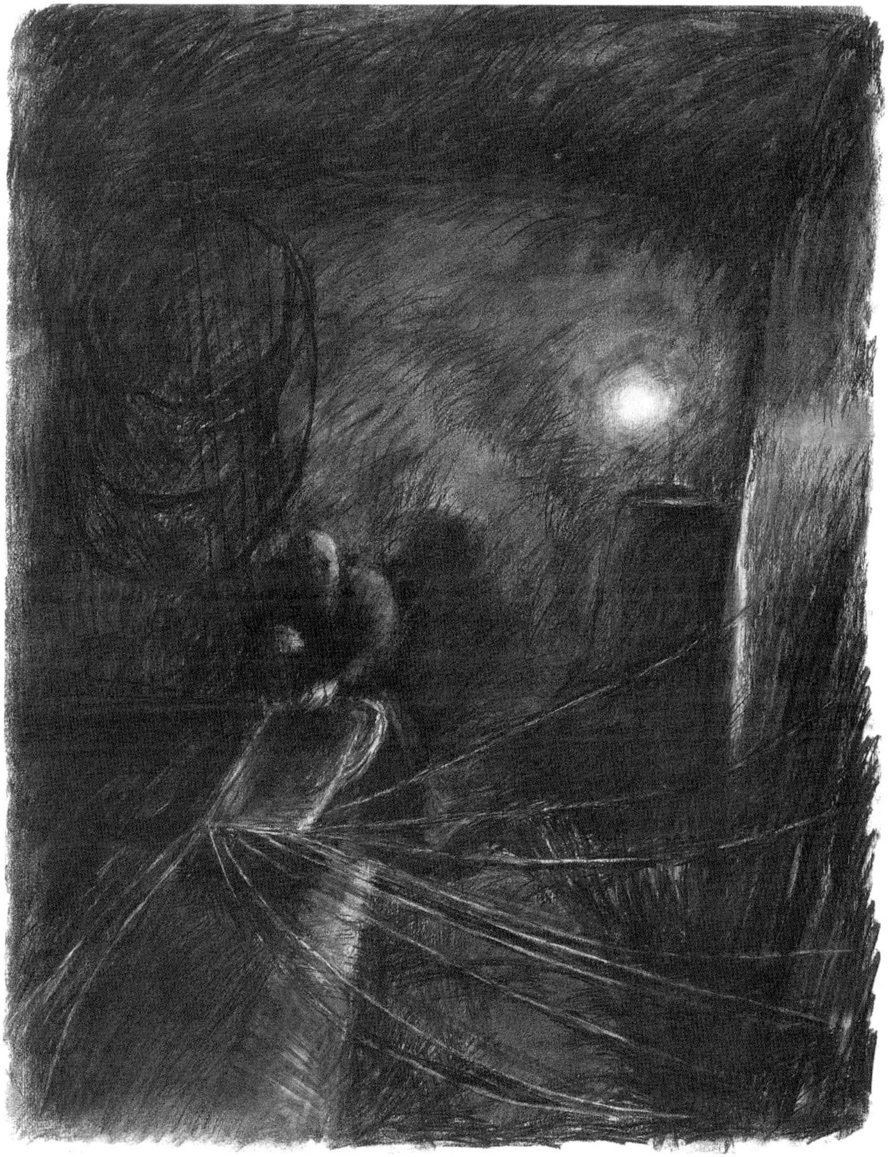

"I'm making a log basket, they call them log baskets now, well you can use them for peat, you can use it for logs, you can use it for anything. Farmers used to use them for feeding their cattle years ago, for putting mangles in that had been pulped up. We used to make an oval one fifteen inches high and twenty one inches long and he was made for putting under the old machines years ago that used to pulp mangles, he would fit in underneath and slide out. And the picker baskets, you used to make a twenty pound and a forty pound and a thirty pound, oh yes, there were all different sizes, loads of different sizes."

IVOR HANCOCK
basketmaker
North Petherton

Ivor Hancock bordering down the foot of a root basket

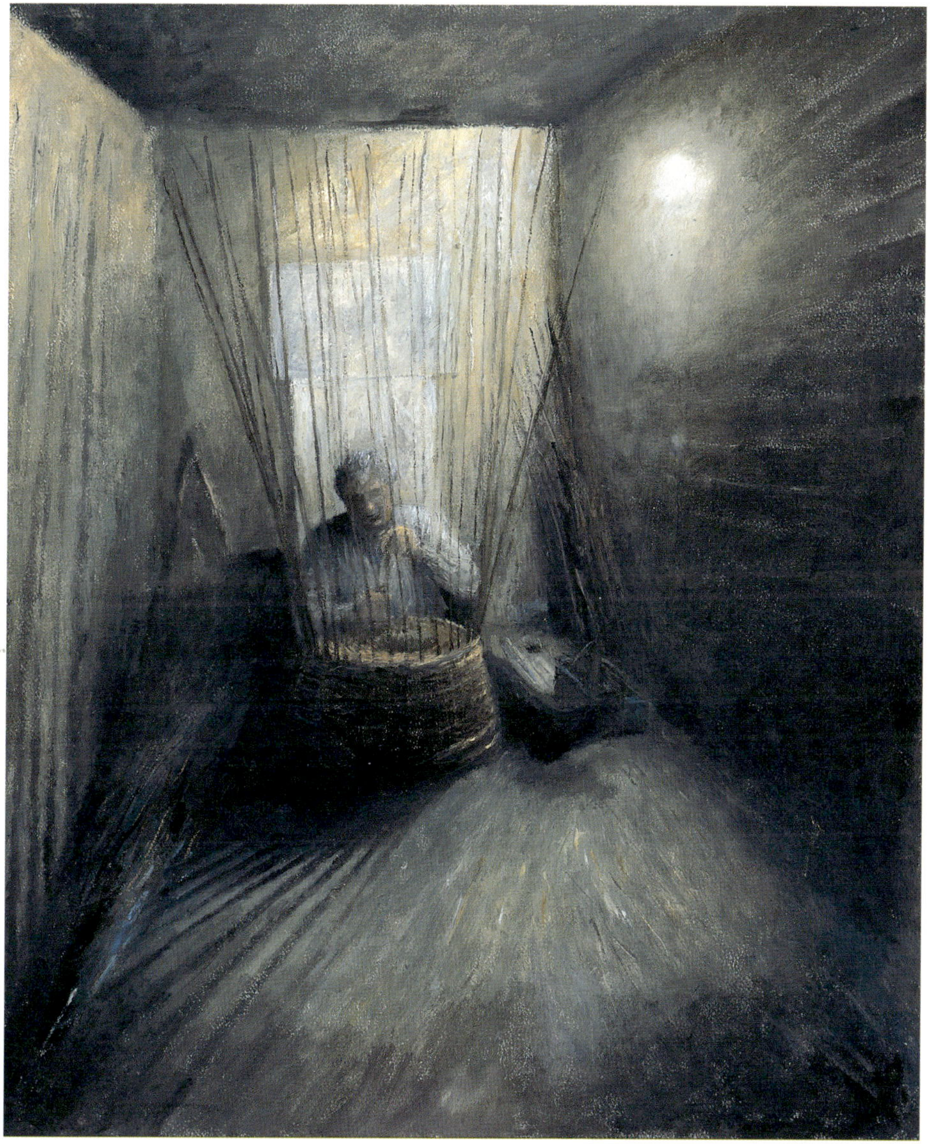

"Bill Bailey came down from Birmingham way and he specialised in pigeon baskets for all the pigeon fanciers, he was a pigeon fancier himself. I did my basic training there. I was mainly on bottoms all the time, making bottoms for a year. I was seventeen and I did a year just making straight-forward bottoms to get used to the feel of willows. I cut my teeth on laundry baskets actually, that was real big heavy work.

Rather than stop and pick up an iron we use our hands and bump the withies down and therefore it gets like elephant hide on the side, it gets really hard. That's another thing, it's hard on the hands because they're all damp, they're all immersed in water before I can make them pliable. It's best not to use them soaking wet, but they're all damp, so if you get a cold and frosty morning then it's not so good then on the hands."

PETE NICHOLAS
basketmaker
Stathe

Pete Nicholas upsetting

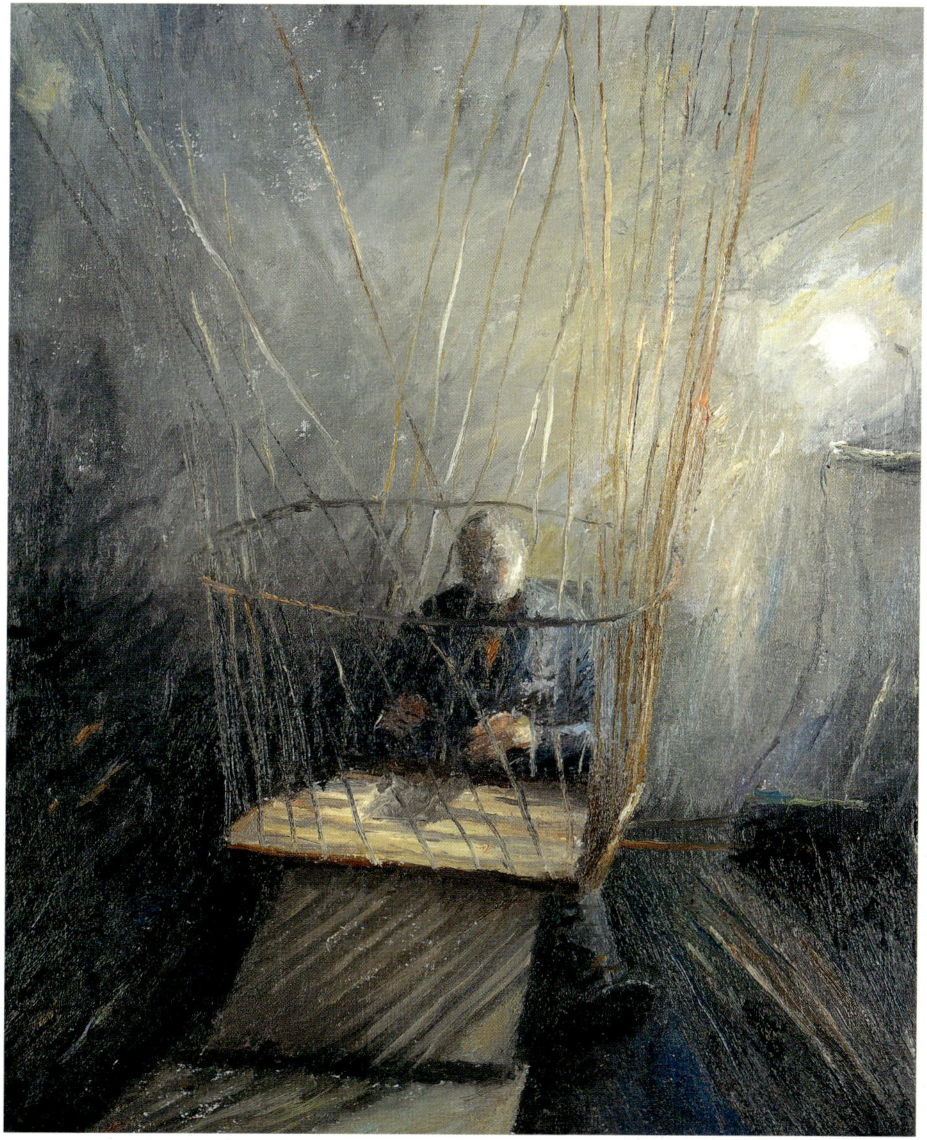

"We were making pigeon baskets for quite a few years. It gradually faded out, but other things seemed to come in, like the fishing baskets and we made thousands and thousands of picnic baskets. We did have a few strange requests, an illusionist came in and wanted a basket made in the shape of an Ali Baba jar so that his very pretty assistant could go inside and he could push swords through. Then I had a phone call one day and the voice said 'can you make large laundry baskets?' and I said 'yes, we can make anything', being very big-headed about it, and the guy turned up with a balloon basket on a trailer behind a little MG and said 'can you make one of these?' and that's when it started, about twenty five years ago, and it grew from there"

AUBREY HILL
Somerset Willow Company
Bridgwater

Aubrey Hill randing and waling a balloon basket

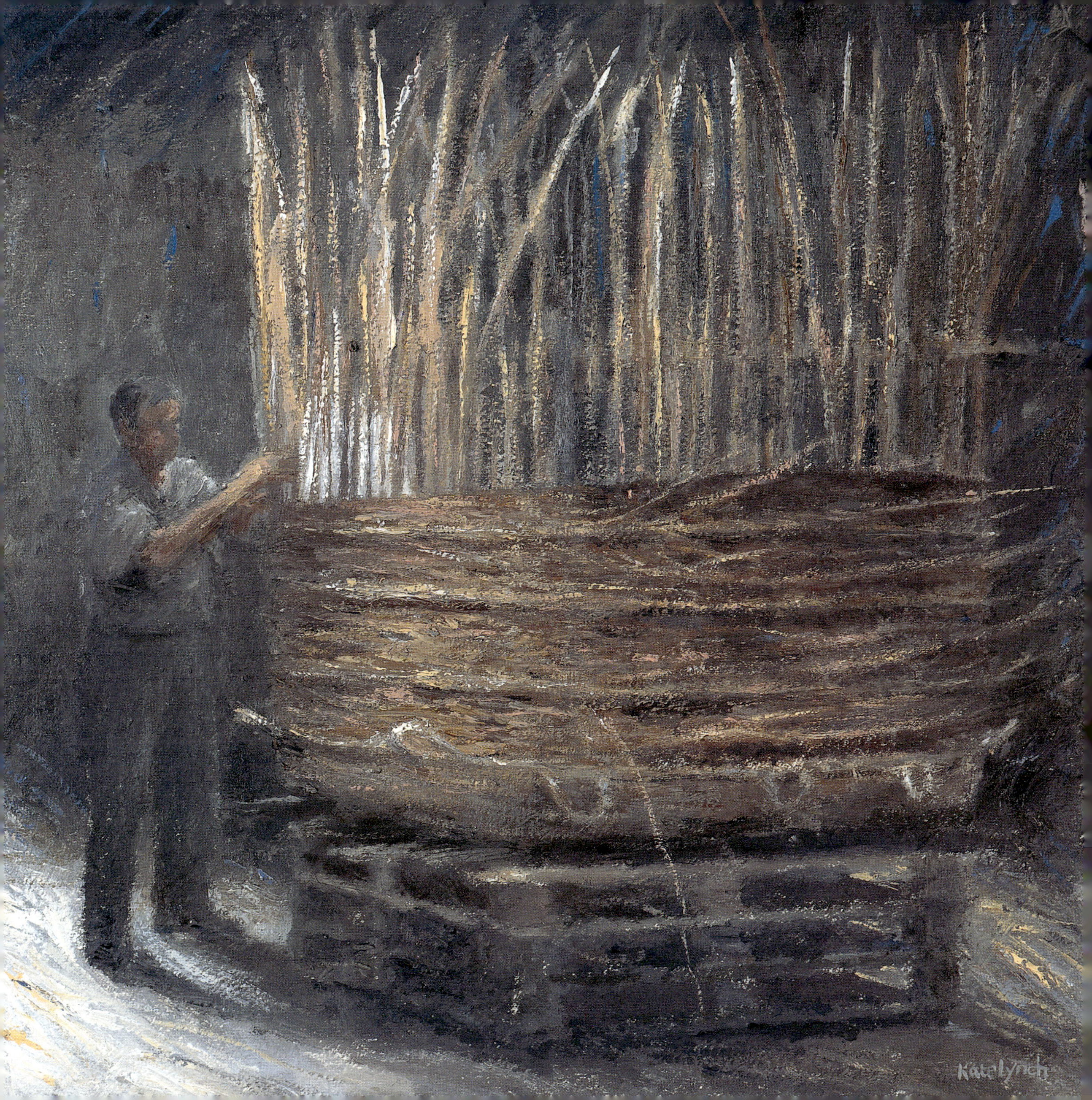
Kate Lynch

"This is the traditional position because everything's on hand, you see if you were sat up to a table you'd spend half your time bending over looking for your tools. After you've made the base it's what's called staking up, a sharp tool, a bodkin, you press through the outside stick, and then put the stake into the hole that you've made....a cow horn, you put grease in there to grease the bodkin, but when you're on piece work, you haven't always got the time to do that, so you find it easier to rub it through your hair, if you've got some! After it's been staked up you upset, and they used to tell me that if you don't upset it properly it will upset you before you finish! It's the same weave as a wale, a three rod wale, using three willows, which is the foundation of the basket. The single rod rand is another weave and this will take the side of the basket up, then I'll do a wale around the top which'll serve as a foundation for the finish of the basket, the border, which is a different process again."

PETE NICHOLAS
basketmaker
Stathe

Pete Nicholas bordering down

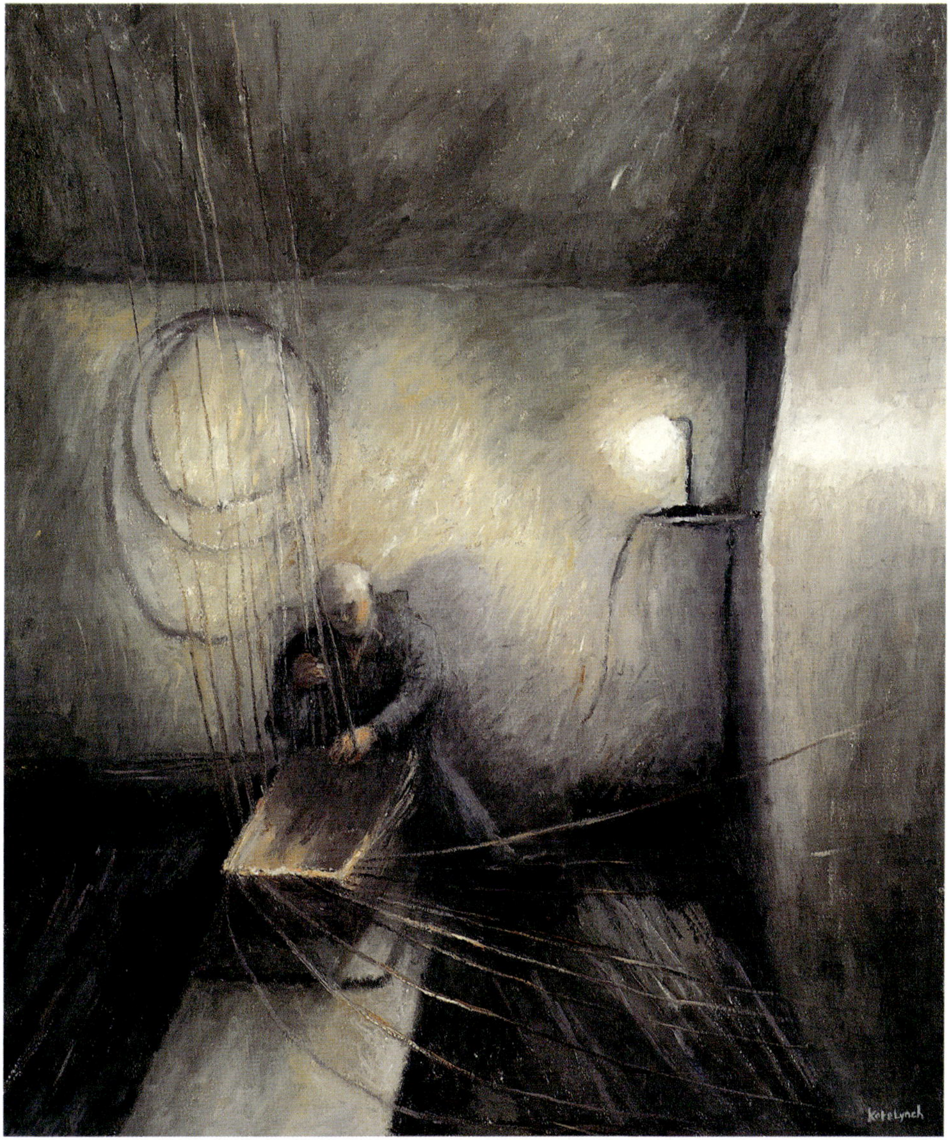
KateLynch

"I make anything that's put in front of me, magazine racks, waste paper baskets, shopping baskets, flower baskets of different shapes and sizes, children's shopping baskets, you name it, I do it. I think my Dad would be shocked that I'd be the only one left doing it, I don't think he thought I'd ever make a basketmaker, but I've proved him wrong."

MARY NASH
basketmaker
Stoke St Gregory

Mary Nash French-randing steamed willow

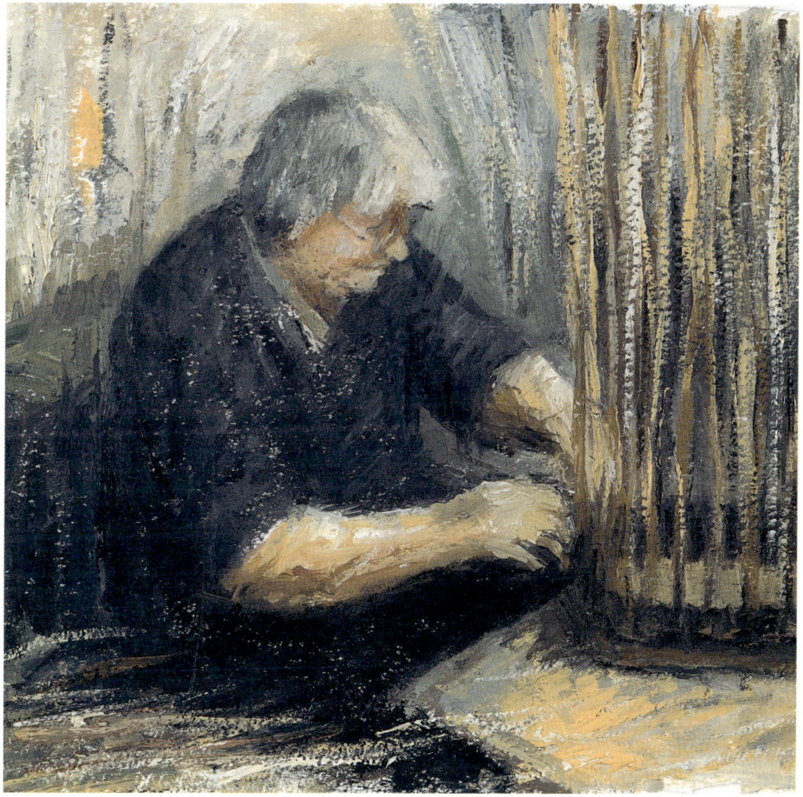

"A peck basket would be oval in shape. It was sturdily made and nearly everyone living in the villages used to have one of these because they used to dig their own gardens and grow their own vegetables and that was the most useful basket. There were twenty pounders and thirty pounders and a forty pounder would be a flower pot shape with a handle either side and a sixty and an eighty pounder. They needed to be made strong 'cos they had a lot of rough use. Peck baskets were used for apple picking. We used to make domestic baskets, cribs, shopping baskets, linen baskets and all kinds you know, butt baskets, withy butts, coal merchants used to use them, and for peat as well. Fishing baskets, you don't get asked for many of those, whereas years ago, if anyone went fishing they weren't a fisherman unless they had a willow basket. The use of baskets has changed. What farmers wanted was something strong and durable, not particularly fancy to look at. The thing about Somerset baskets, they're still made strong."

ALF BREWER
basketmaker
Ashcott

Alf Brewer randing a kitchen basket

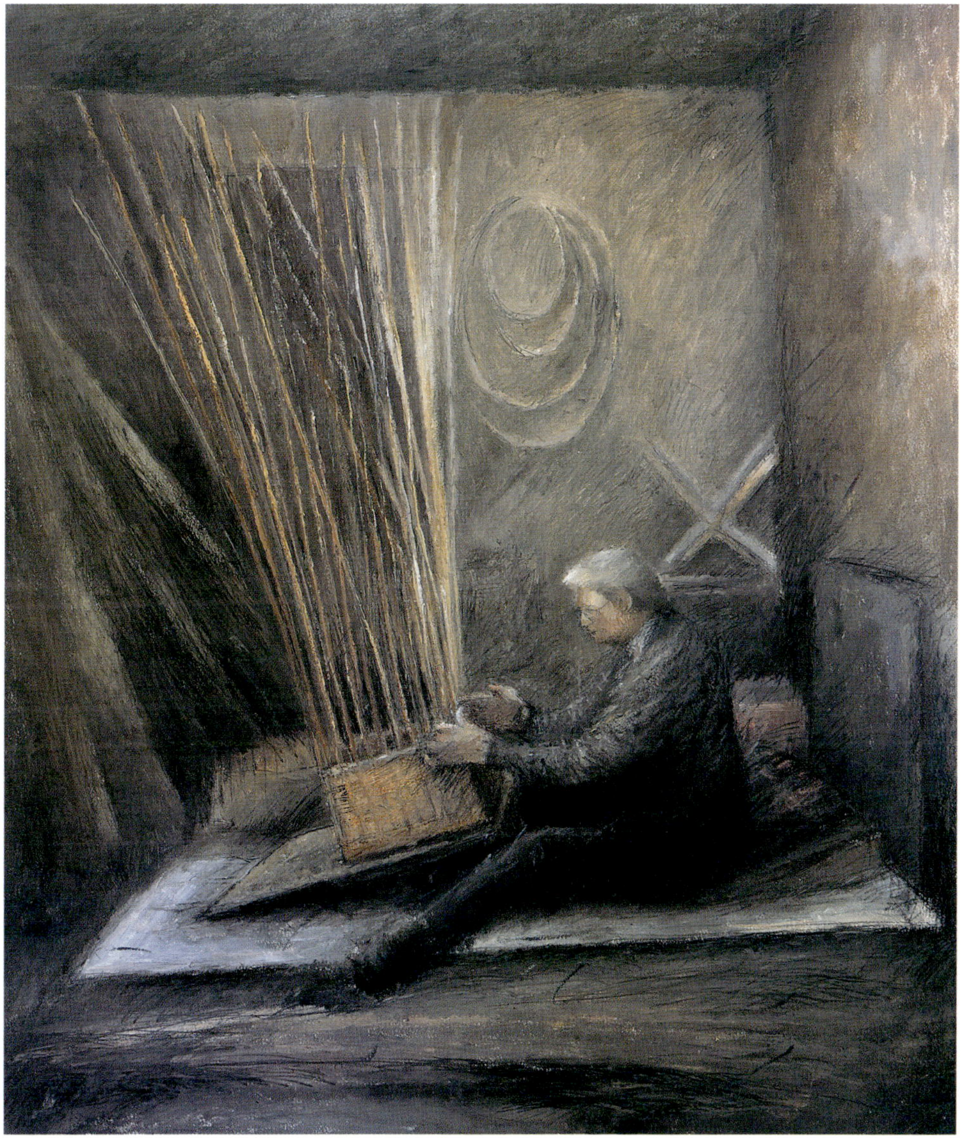

"When a woven balloon basket hits the ground it gives and seems to spring back into shape and up until now they've found nothing to take its place. One of the most exciting things was, I had to make a balloon basket to break the world record for the most number of people and it carried fifty people and was built like a double-decker bus, with a basket on top of the first one, with a ladder between the two, and that did indeed break the world record.

It takes a certain kind of person to be able to make baskets, it's not a clean job by any means and it's hard work and unfortunately these days people like to press buttons and use computers. Strangely enough, it's surprising how long basketmakers keep working and they seem to thrive on it, and I can tell you now that as long as I'm healthy enough I will always work."

AUBREY HILL
Somerset Willow Company
Bridgwater

Aubrey Hill, randing and waling a balloon basket

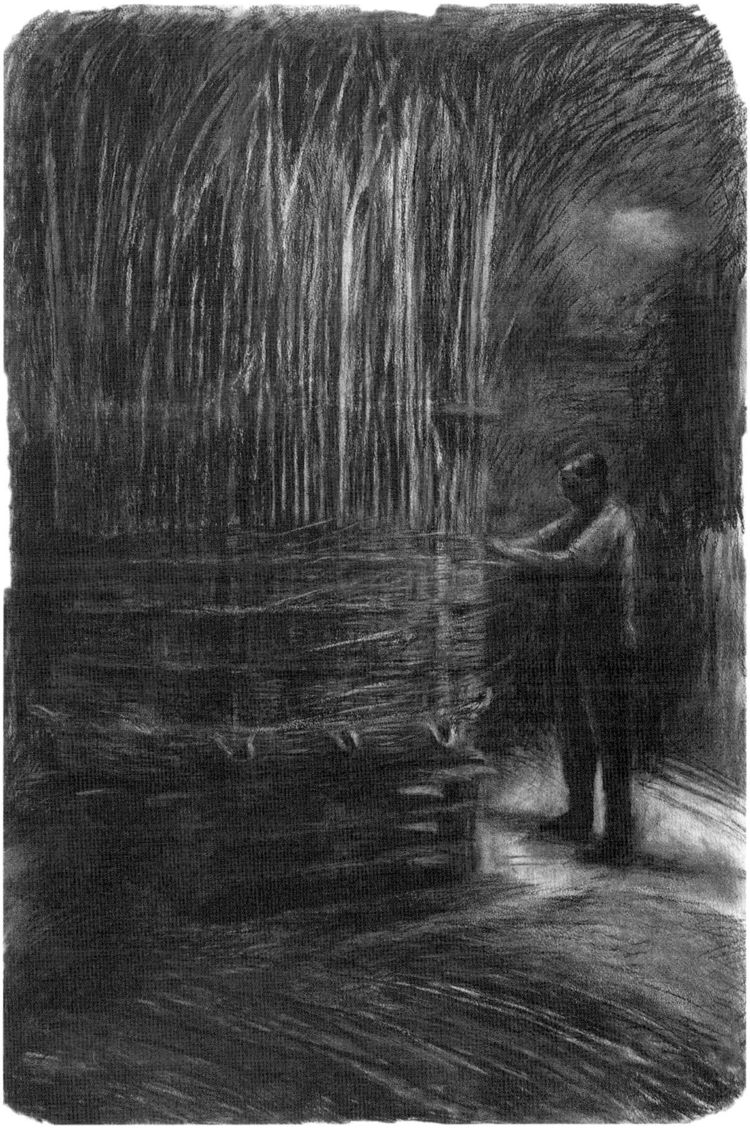

"All willows feel different because the soil changes, you get some willows that feel light, others feel heavy. It's a strange thing to explain. It's a natural material which is just fantastic to use. Oh, to begin with it's murder, it really is. When I first started I can remember thinking 'I'll never last!' You get back ache because you are leaning over the basket, your legs ache because they are pushed down by the weight of the board, the basket and the iron, and your ankles ache because your ankles are out at angles. It's a hard thing to get used to and your hands split. In the winter, there's ice on them, wet, it's horrible, they just crack. But it's the same as any job, there's down sides, but, once you get used to it, the pluses outweigh the bad things to be honest. We're never going to get rich doing this. I do it because I love making baskets. I've been doing it for nineteen years and I still wake up every morning looking forward to what I'm going to do."

MIKE HUBBARD
basketmaker
Chedzoy

Mike Hubbard making a bottom

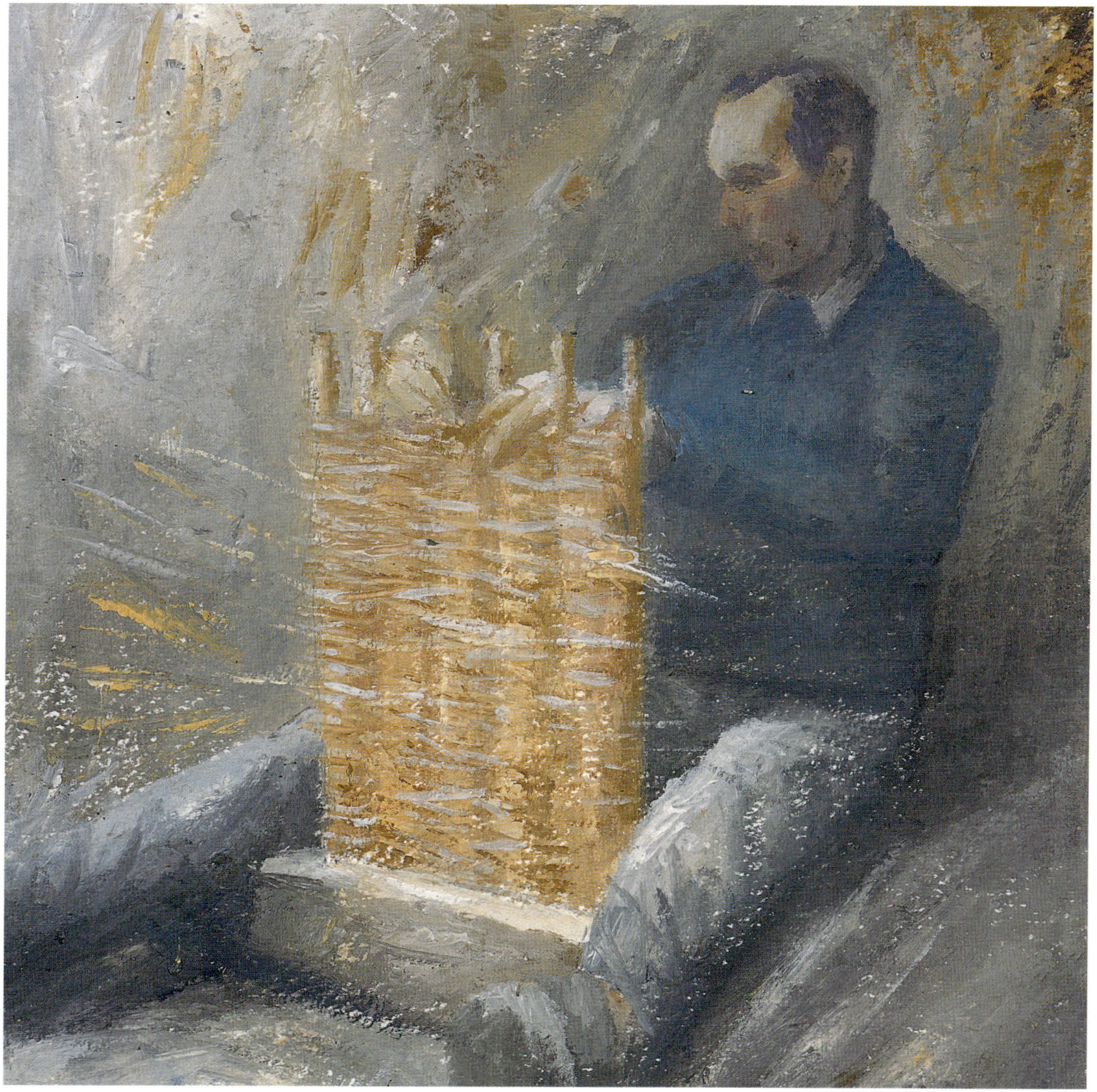

"Basketwork coffins go back thousands of years. We first started weaving coffins about six years ago, someone asked us, and people just seem to love the idea. We're making them all the time now and there's some interest from the States. They're hand-made from a local material, and I suppose there's more of a personal touch, they're individual, softer to look at. It's surprising how much interest there is in something people don't normally talk about, it brings a smile to their faces."

DARRELL HILL
Somerset Willow Company
Bridgwater

Andy Hill bordering down a coffin

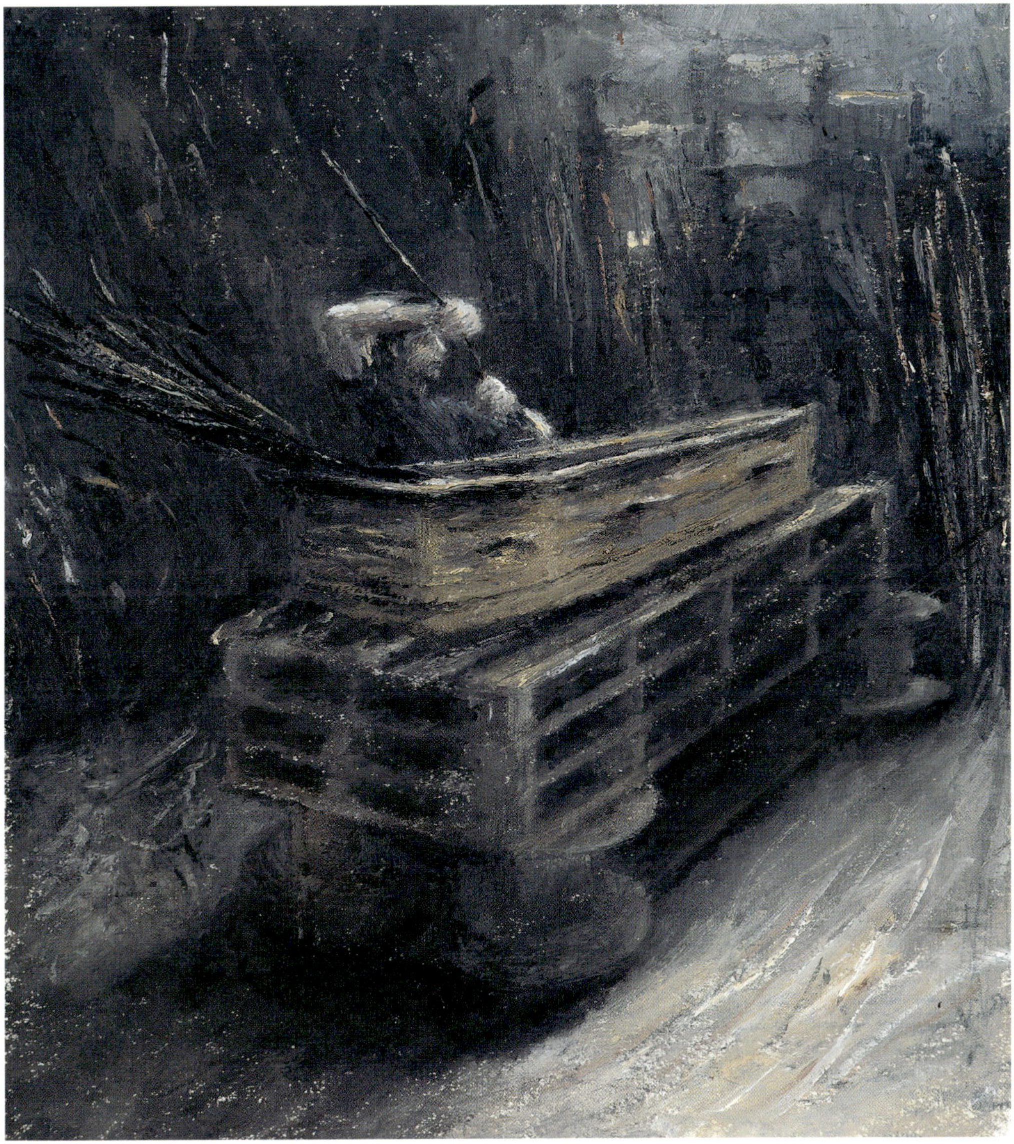

SCULPTURE, STRUCTURES, BATS AND SPARS

"It had to be something that welcomed people into the area, I decided it was better to have him running into the south rather than running out. We started on the bottom and worked our way up to the top, to the shoulders. There's hoops on the framework so that's creating a volume of forms and, with willow, wind passes through it, and it's one of those odd things that the heavier the thing becomes the more stable it is. I'm not art and I'm not craft, I'm somewhere in the middle and I'm surrounded by a work force of crafts people who make baskets and hurdles for a living. It's good, it keeps your feet firmly on the ground."

SERENA DE LA HEY
sculptor
Curload

Serena, four storeys up, weaving Willow Man

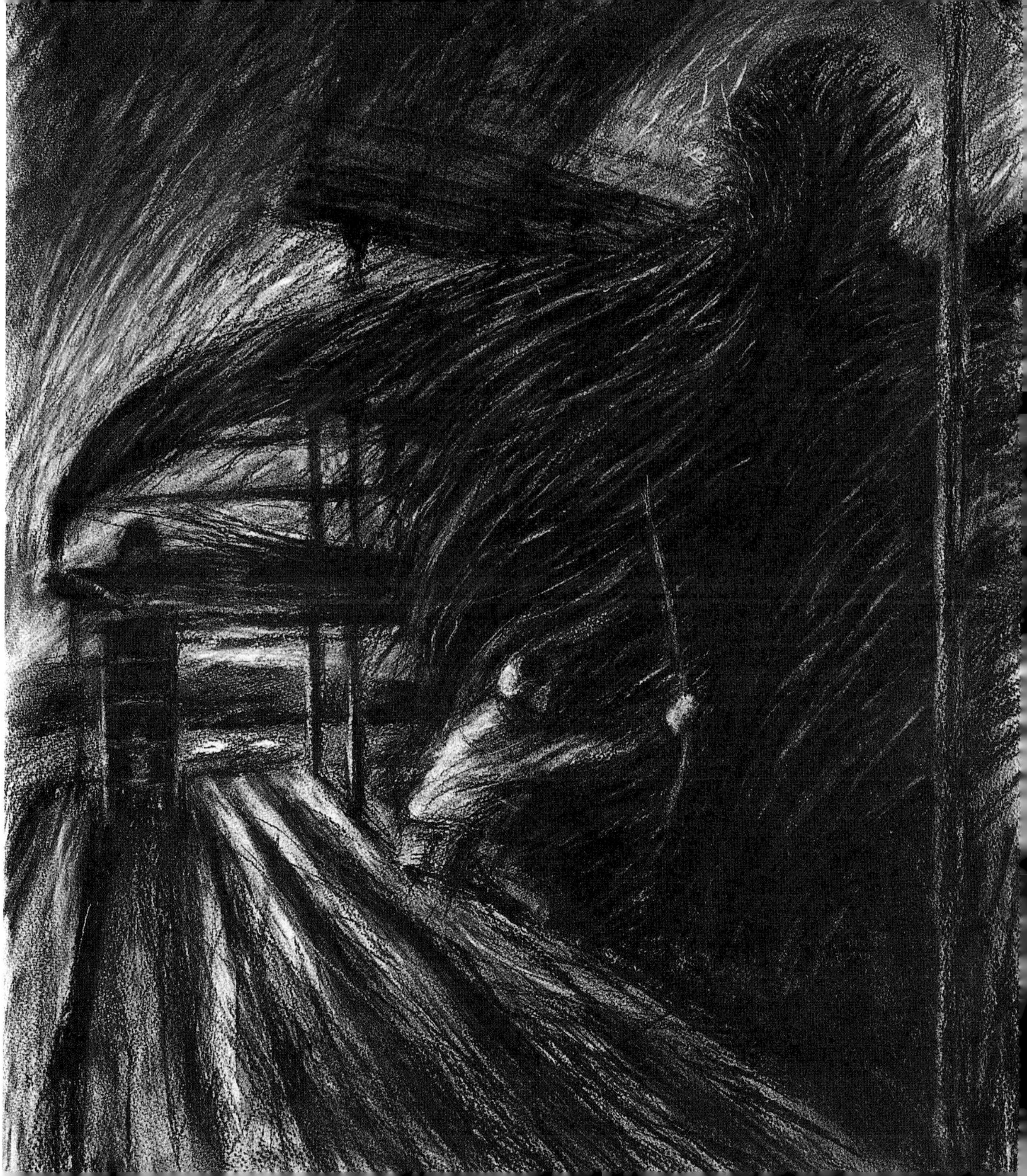

"The hurdle side I was taught when I first came here, from Stan Dare, he was the one who worked here where I am now. I've been here for the best part of seventeen years. I make a variety, anything really, arbours, arches, gates, hurdles, six-foots. These are about two years' growth, they've gone in the boiler for about three hours just to soften them, so they stay flexible then for three or four days. Willow bank work is different, it's from Christmas time right through up until May, spiling is what we call the actual river bank weaving, with living willows. It's generally on the corner where the water is running down from the straight, you're up to your waist, it's a bit cold at times. You get to go to different places, the last job was at Chester, that went on for about four weeks. It's nice, I quite enjoy it."

ANDY COX
hurdlemaker and river bank weaver
Curload

Andy Cox, slewing a hurdle

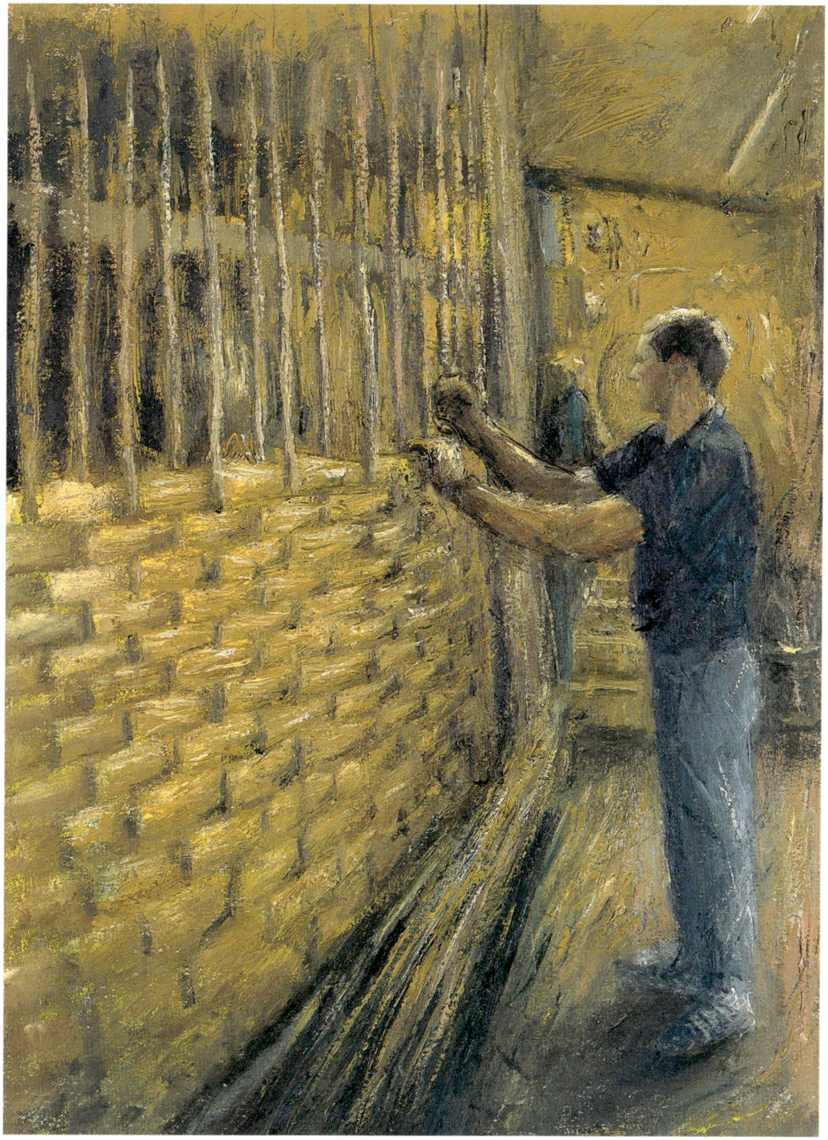

"Mr Champion, he was a relation of mine, he was in his eighties and he came to teach us, he lived over at Lyng, Albert Champion. He was a furniture maker. You've got to be a certain standard, so people know your work, people know what they want. You've got imported baskets coming in, people think they're a little bit cheaper, but in some cases they're not what they expect. My shoppers, I see them, probably ones I made when I first started, they last for years".

CHRIS BECK
basketmaker
Curload

Chris Beck slewing the sides of a bower seat

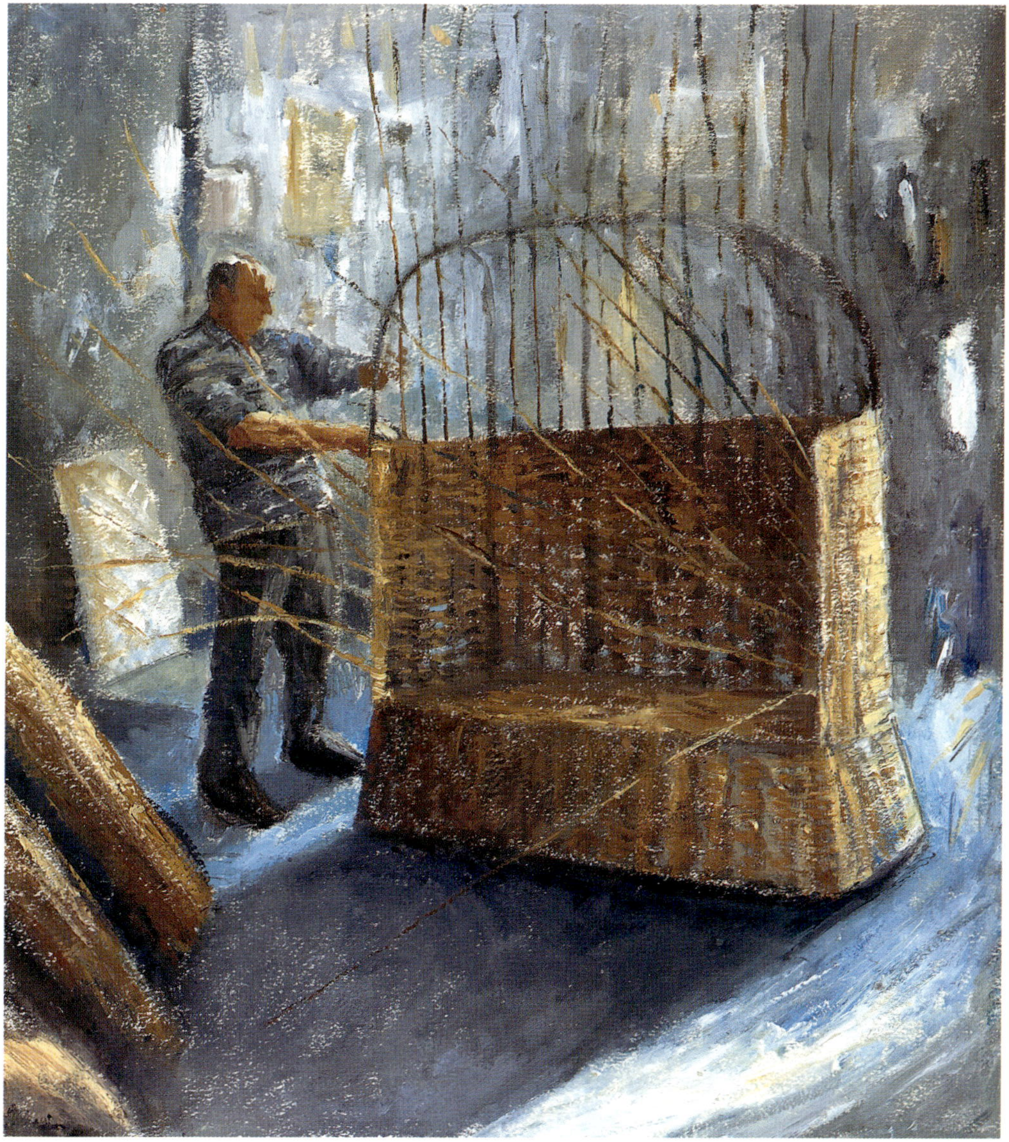

"You can make them from withies or hazel wood, but mostly withies, which used to be plenty years ago, but not so plentiful today because when the rick thatching died out farmers thought spars won't be wanted and cut the trees down, which was a big mistake because you still need thousands of spars for house thatching. It needs a small sharp hook, and very sharp, it must be sharp to put the point on because each stick is split out. You've got a point at each end, and when you use it for thatching you have to twist it in the middle to form like a hairpin which pegs the thatching into the roofs. We could make a thousand a day in the heydays, but I find now withies don't split so well as they did forty, fifty years ago, because I think we're getting so many mild winters without severe weather that the sap is still in the sticks all winter."

HAROLD WRIGHT
spar maker (retired thatcher)
Compton Dundon

Harold Wright making willow spars in his greenhouse

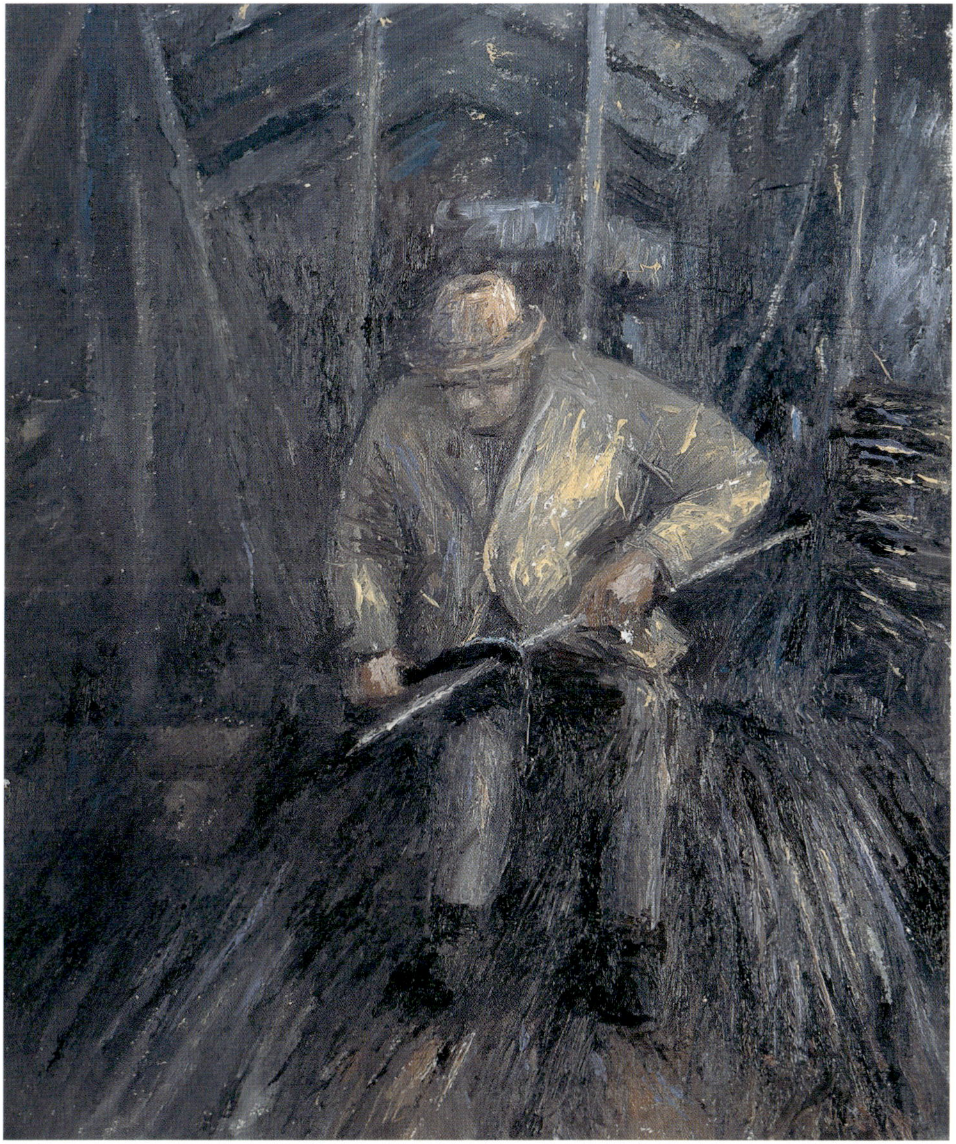

"I use cultivated willow from the Somerset Levels. It's the most remarkable natural resource, with properties and qualities superior to any synthetic materials. I think of it as an elastic hardwood with tremendous tensile strength and delicacy of line and a variety of finish and colour that are totally natural. In my stick chairs I use it with ash poles, thinned from Dorset woodland, they provide the contrast and structure for the delicate lines of the wind blown willow. In their simple humility these materials capture a truth which touches us all. My approach comes from a vernacular tradition where the techniques and skills evolved from local needs and materials, but my furniture is also informed by modern life and technology."

GUY MARTIN
furniture designer-maker
Crewkerne

Guy Martin, music stand and chair, white stripped willow

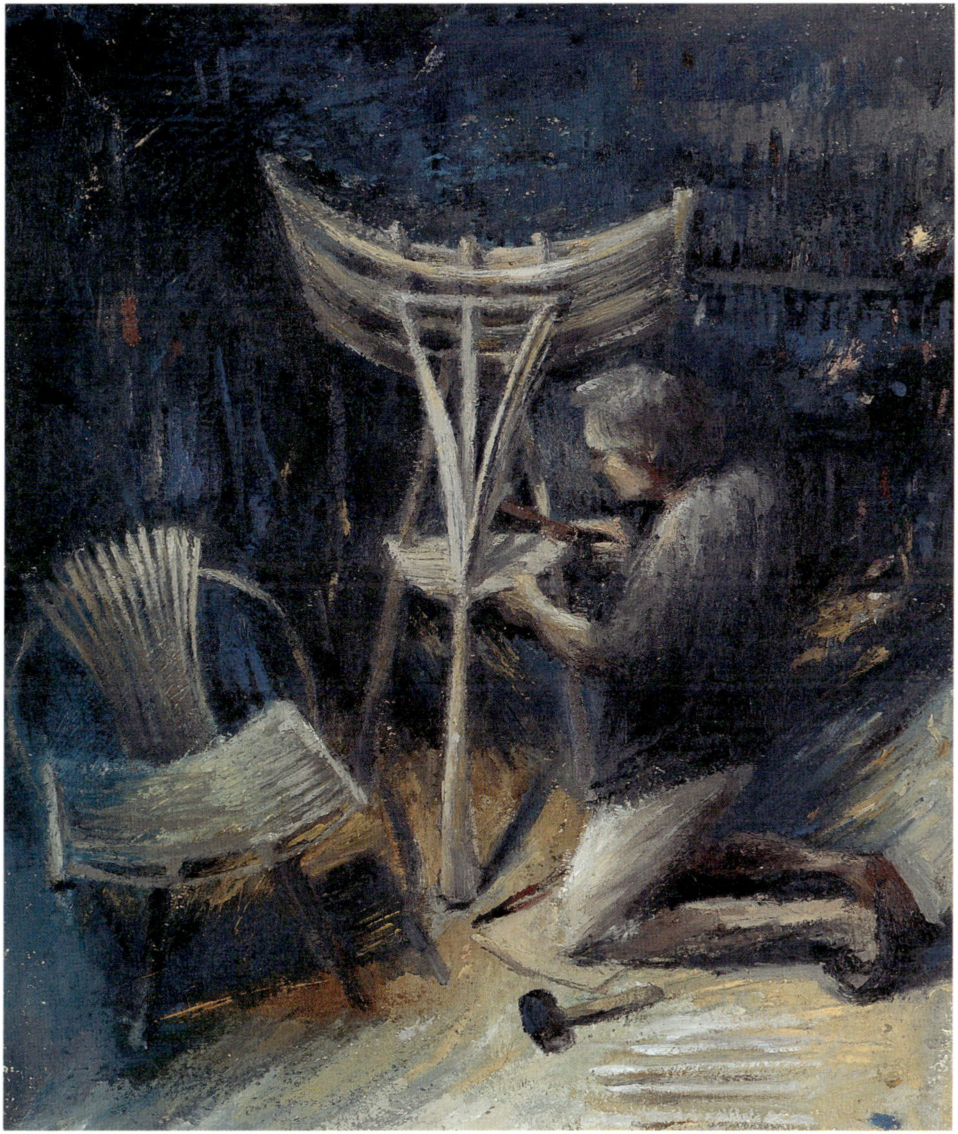

"They are made of willow, English willow. Our bats aren't cheap, but the customer is getting something which is slightly different. Attention to detail, balance, how it feels in the hand is the most important factor. If you can make something that's actually quite heavy feel light, then you're doing well. That's the key. Probably the most important thing people look for, customers would be looking for, something with a clean face, a big profile and something that feels like a feather. That is what people are looking for. I work six days a week, seven in the summer sometimes. It's a good job. I enjoy it."

ROB CHAMBERS
cricket bat maker
Taunton

Rob Chambers with bats in the drying cupboard

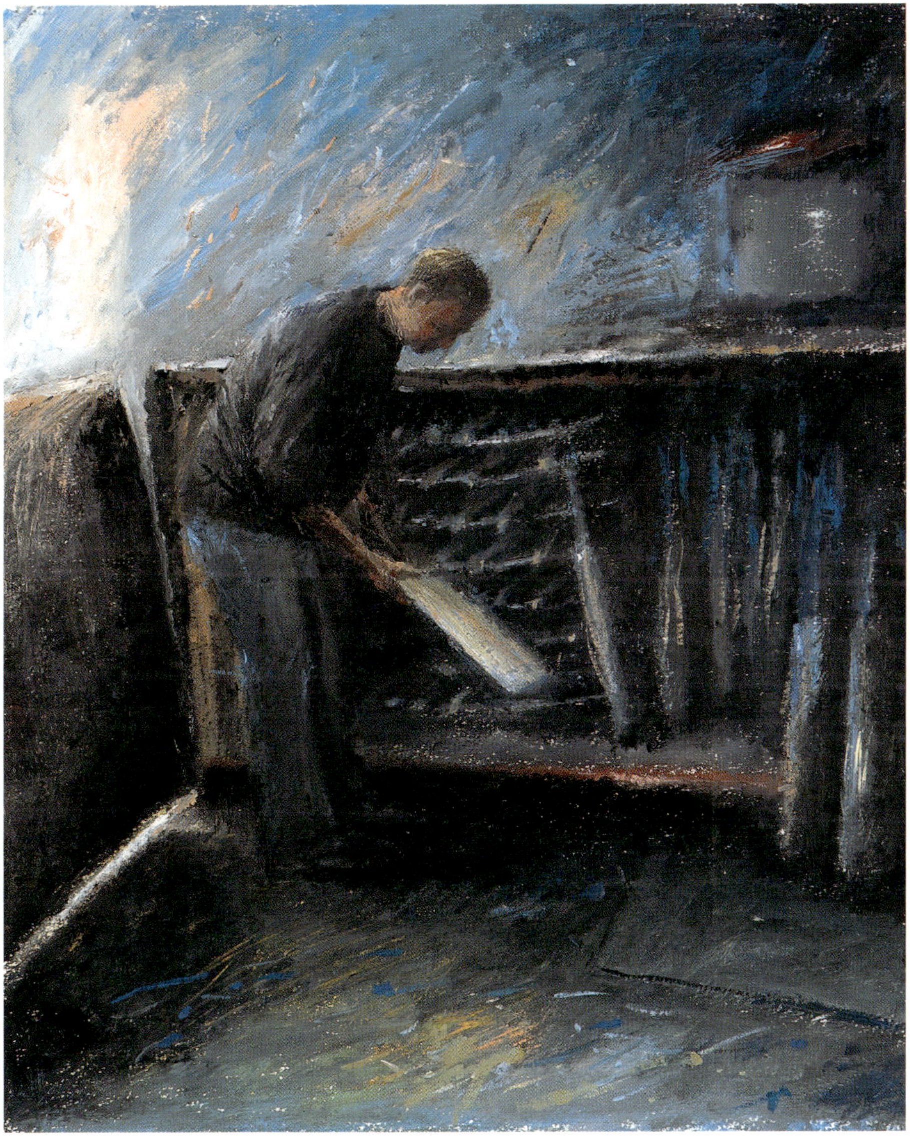

"The handle of the turf scythe was made of goat willow, what we call dun willow. It used to grow out of the bank of peat, came out of the vertical bank. It had a natural curve and we used to put it into the cutting tool. Also the willow is soft to handle, not like ash or hickory, it was quite comfortable to use. You probably had it in your hands for the biggest part of the day. The curve is quite unique, you can look over the top of it and see where you're cutting. Then we'd use willow baskets, hawking baskets, to carry the turves round to the houses. There was a chap lived at Bawdrip, a basketmaker, I think his name was Mr. Stone, he was blind, and it was incredible. Father would want baskets made and they were always exactly the same size. Then we went on to logs and Father always used to get him to make the handles extra strong 'cos we were using them all the time."

ROGER ROGERS
former peat digger

Roger Rogers digging peat, Westhay

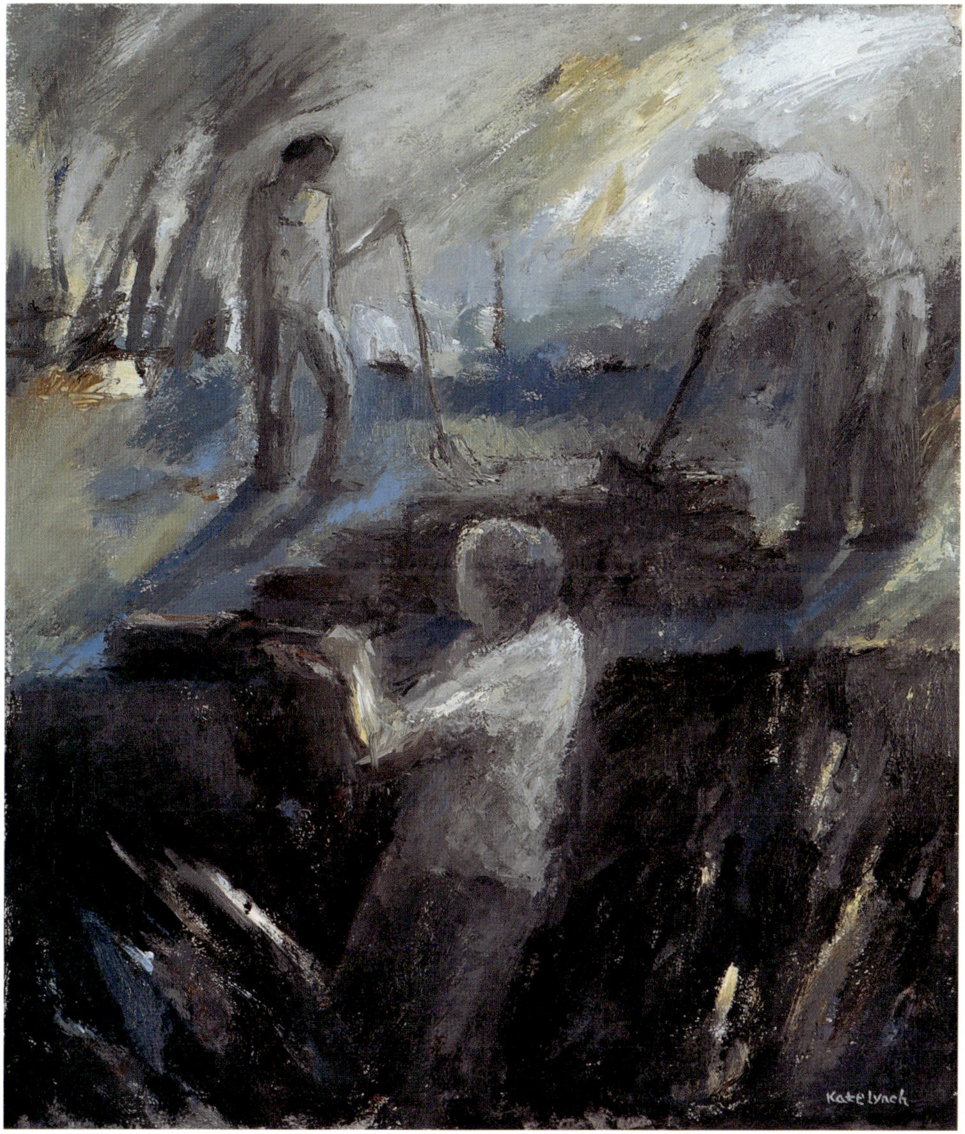
Kate Lynch

WILLOW AND WATER

"In recent years we have moved into erosion control on rivers, where we put willow stakes into the riverbanks and weave living willow between them during the winter and the whole lot grows and stabilises the banks. We are a green and soft solution. It is nothing new. I think man was doing it when he was living in very primitive times in wattle shelters. I think he protected his bit of bank for his ducks the same as we do it now. The stakes are harvested from the crop from the beginning of November, when the leaf is off the tree, they are pushed into the riverbed, and in between we weave living willow, then in the Spring the stakes and the weave grow. The whole technique is called willow spiling. This year we will run two teams, if not three. It is lovely dealing with a business that people want and enjoy and is beneficial to the environment".

NIGEL HECTOR
English Hurdle
Curload

Andy Cox and Ray Winchester river bank spiling, mid-Somerset

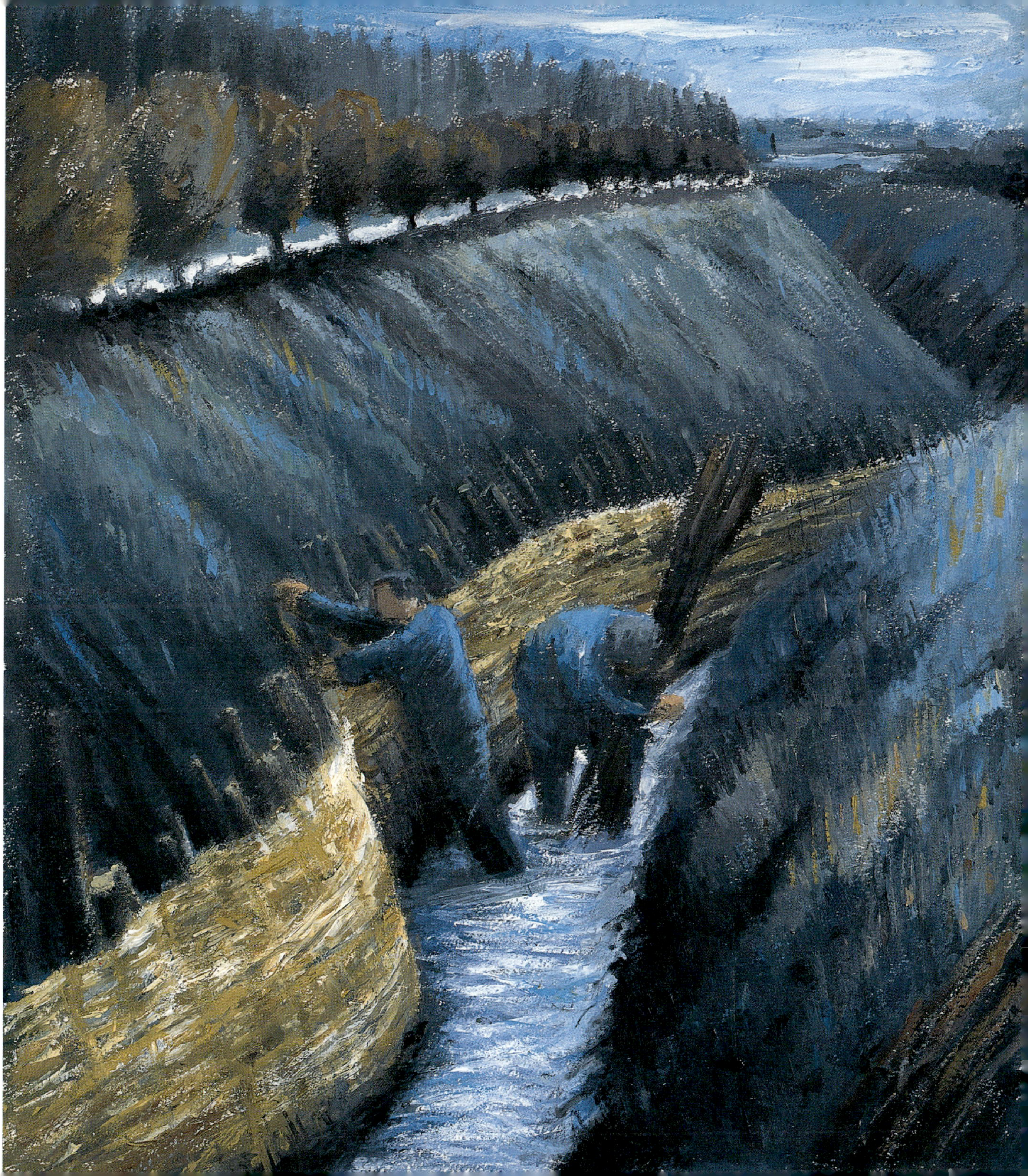

"We always used to get them out on the Levels, there was always a lot of people made baskets and we got our reaps and willy baskets and score baskets and picker baskets. Everybody had willows, always had the willows. The reaps are to cool the shrimps in, nice big round reaps, about four feet across. My dad used to have two or three dozen of them all up the side of the house and when we had big catches of shrimps he'd just tip 20 or 30 pound in a basket and they'd be all steaming and then they'd dry off nice and they'd nearly rattle like nuts. The basket is very old and has been used for so long, it's still very effective and does the job properly. Well plastic is alright, but the basket, the old willow basket is really the best for doing the job."

BRENDAN SELLICK
mud horse fisherman
Stolford

Brendan Sellick cooling hot shrimps in willow reap

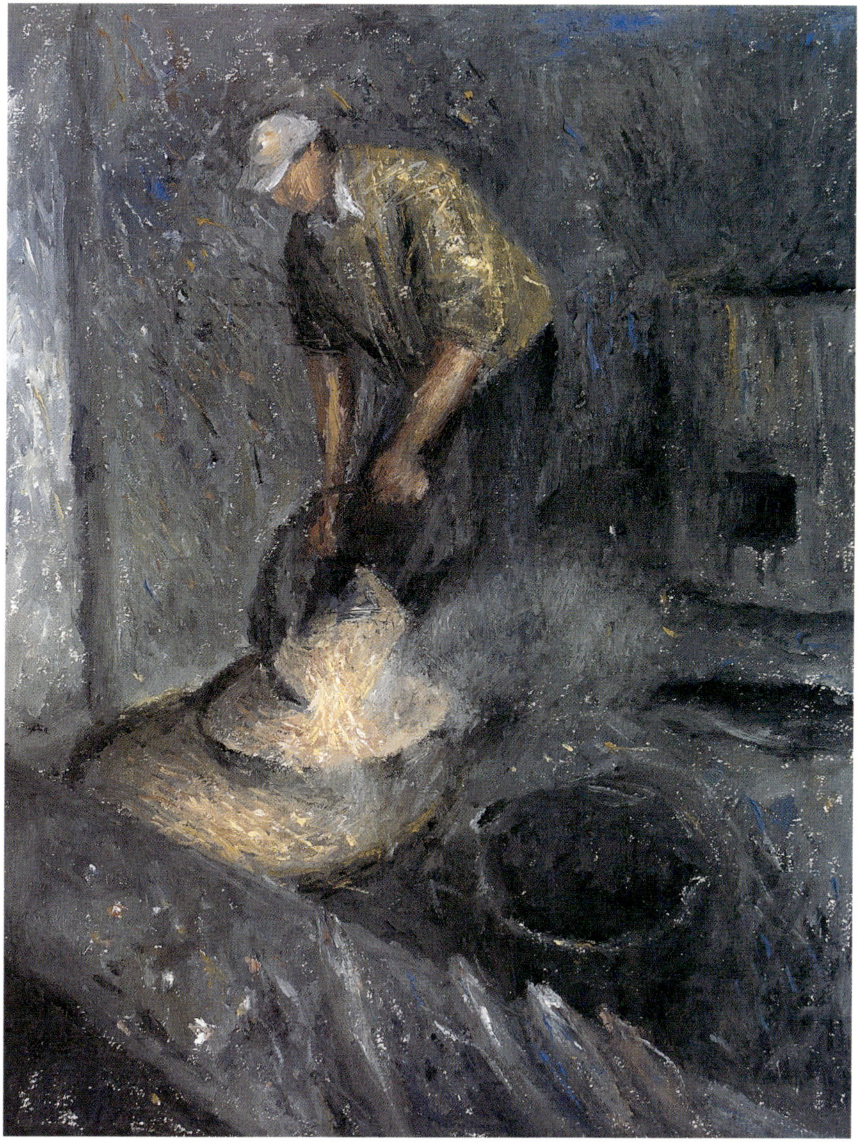

"My father would sit me in the basket when I was small. One particular time stands out when I was on the mud horse about two miles off and I wasn't no more than three years old and my father said 'now, hang on there' and he runned across the mud 'cos a couple of great big conger eels had slipped out of the net and was slithering all across the mud and I can see him now rushing across the mud leaving me on the mud horse and he catching this big conger eel.

The willy basket was the one that the men used to have with a great big leather strap that they used to put on their shoulders and you could put two hundredweight of fish or shrimps in and carry it all across the rocks and up over the beach and the air could get through the withies. That was a big thing with the withies, when you were out there working for several hours, in the hot weather, the shrimps could breathe and the fish could be still kept nice and fresh."

BRENDAN SELLICK
mud horse fisherman
Stolford

Brendan Sellick cooling hot shrimps in willow reap

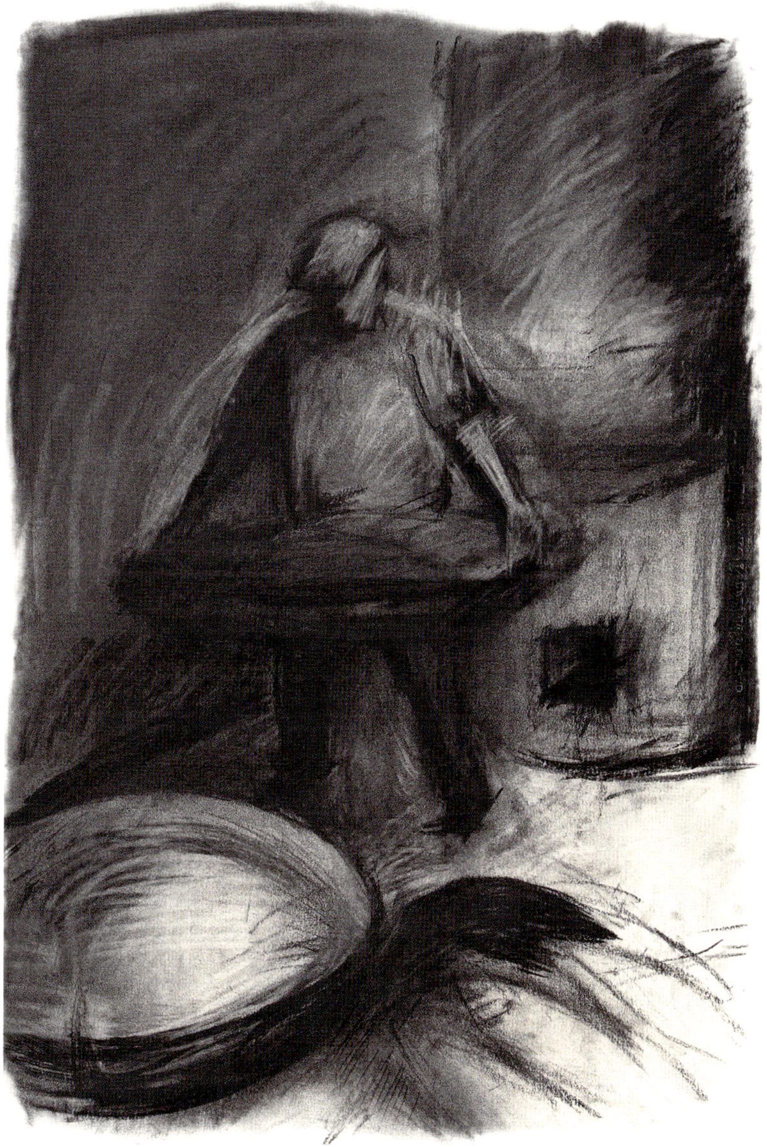

"We used to catch elvers and we used to catch eels as well. Willow eel traps we used to have for catching eels, and salmon traps made from willow, and my grandfather had an old net he made from willow, cut some willow off a tree and made the frame for the net and put some canvas over it and made his own elver net and we used to go out on the river bank and catch the elvers. We used to get sixpence a pint for them back years ago. You'd go out and wait for the tide to turn, put the light behind, you'd catch them at night, it was mainly at night you'd catch them, there aren't many elvers about now, it's over-fished, over-fished."

EDDIE BARNARD
basketmaker
Middlezoy

Elver fisherman, River Parrett

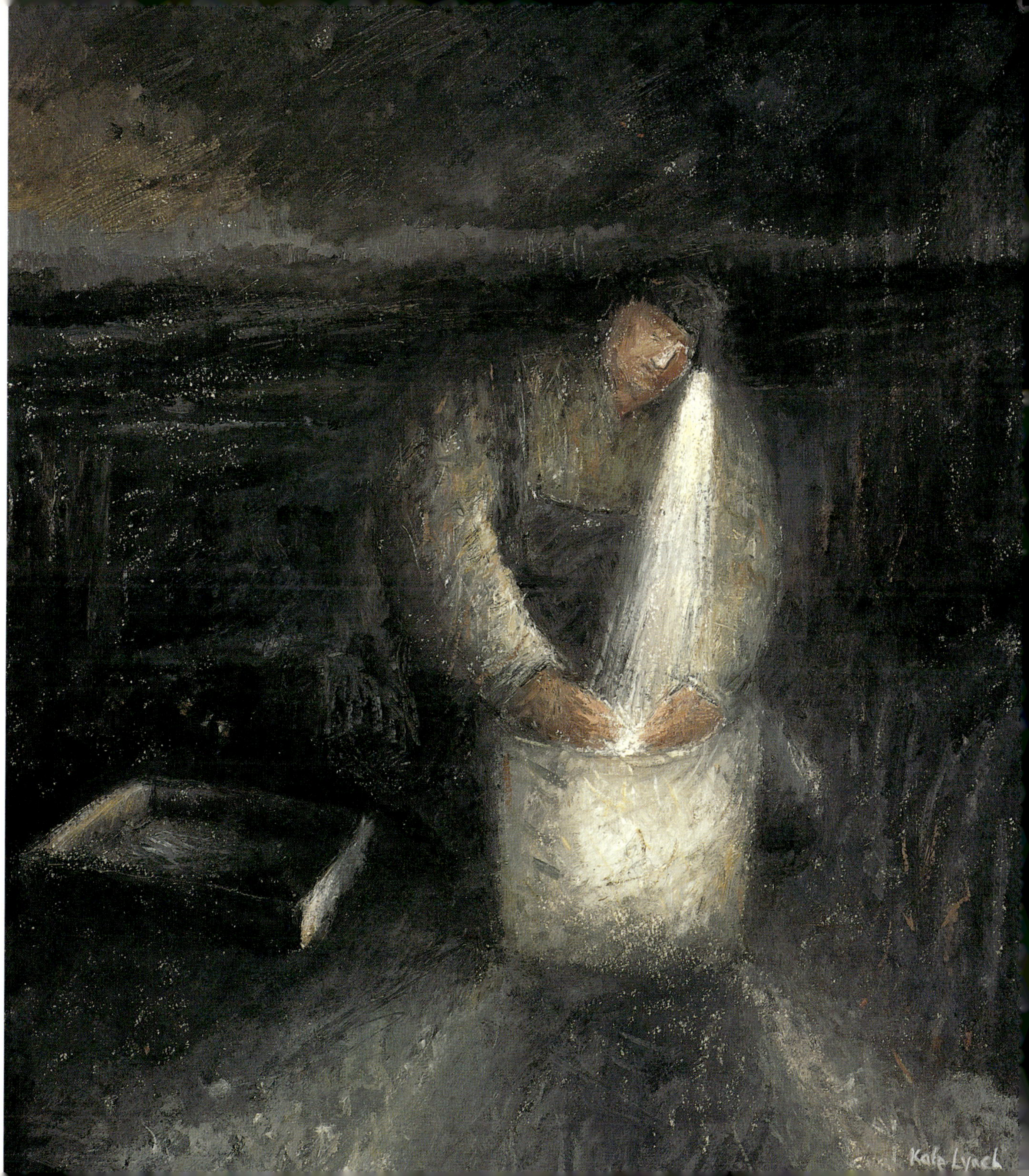
Kate Lynch

AFTERWORD KATE LYNCH

Four years ago we left North Cadbury and moved to the Somerset Levels, only sixteen miles down the road, yet I found myself in a foreign landscape. Gone were the hills I'd grown to love on the Somerset Dorset border and which had provided the inspiration for much of my picture-making and there was talk of cider, peat, withies and eels. I sat and painted the unfamiliar landscape but the pictures lacked passion. I needed to find out whose landscape this was, so I began to ask and took my sketchbook with me.

In getting to know the land, I met the willow growers and basketmakers whose families have farmed this flat, often wet, landscape and hand-crafted its harvest for generations. It's been a three year journey. Reg took me to see George boiling, men harvesting willows at Stathe sent me to Pete, the basketmaker, Alf introduced me to the Derhams, the Derhams sell withies to Aubrey, Aubrey makes shrimp 'reaps' for Brendan and so on. The people and the fascinating traditional work they were doing became my subject matter without my making a conscious decision. I felt honoured to be sitting in their sheds, and, best of all, while I watched them working, they told me the story of willow, and so I travelled with them - out to sea, up in the air, visited palace and cricket pitch, climbed up scaffolding and down into World War trenches, for the history of woven willow is as close to the history of civilisation as you can get. Here on the Somerset Levels woven willow has been found in prehistoric trackways, and walls of huts and baskets from the Iron Age to the Romans, and through the centuries our ancestors have fashioned willow sticks and branches into coracles, fish traps, bee skeps, vessels, furniture, wheelchairs, early aeroplane seats, World War pigeon baskets and airborne panniers.

Still today Somerset willows are woven into the framework beneath the Guards' bearskins, there's a revival in willow coffins, modern balloonists ride the skies in monumental Somerset willow baskets, and now green river bank conservation, garden structures and modern sculpture have been added to the willow repertoire by ingenious growers and makers.

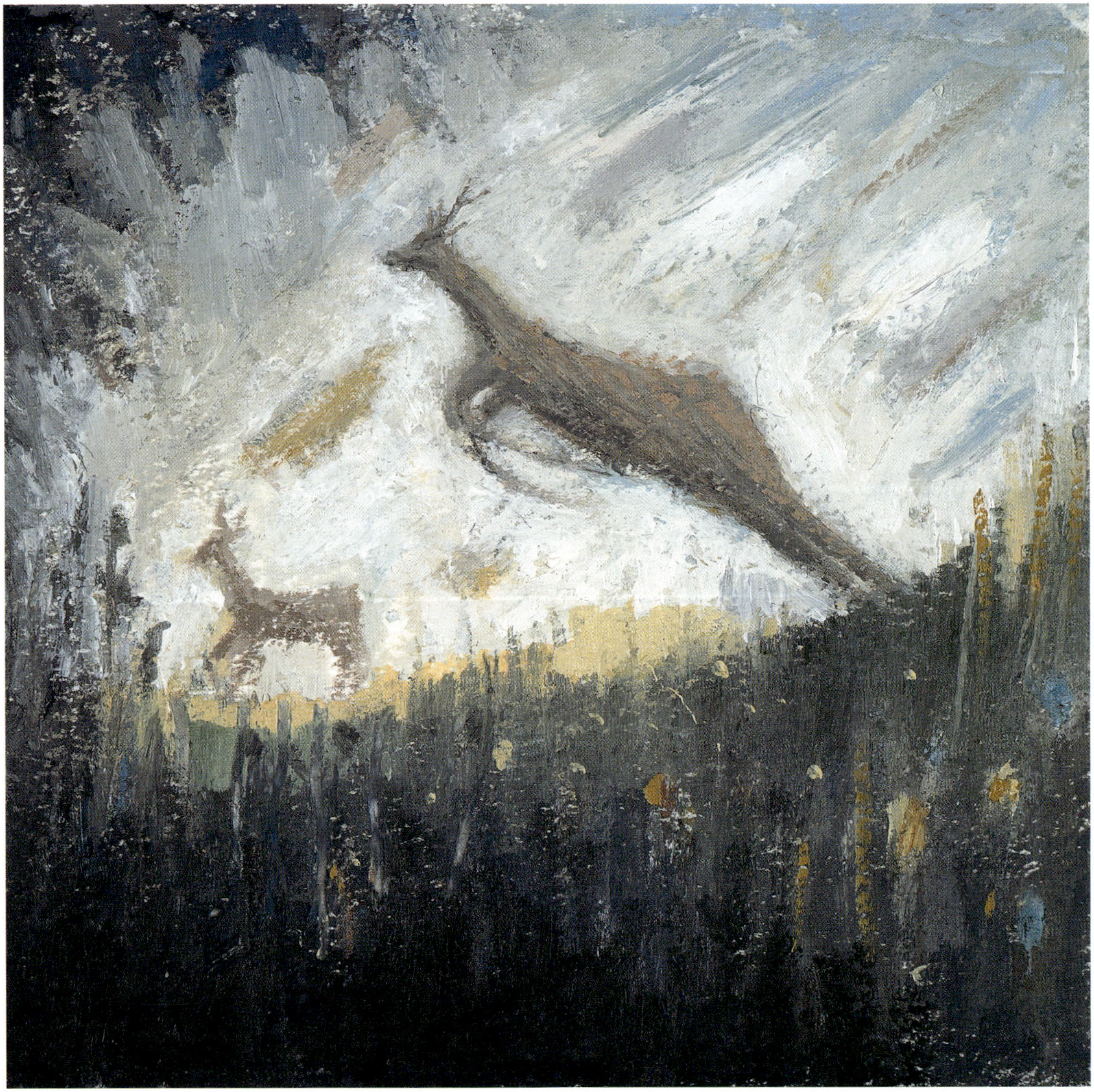

Leaping Roe Deer by Sophie Courtiour and Stefan Jennings

Local basketmaking was commonplace once, in most villages in the country, but in the 19th century far more baskets were needed, burgeoning factories and more deliveries required enormous numbers, and the Victorians loved wicker furniture. There are now machines for some processes, but not for all, and the willow grower can still handle each willow wand individually a dozen times between the first shoots from the stump in April and the selling of a bundle. A small number of traditional Somerset basket-makers survive, where once there were hundreds, and they continue an unbroken tradition of English basketmaking going back generations. So, as I was drawing the local growers and basket-makers, I was not just in the here and now, I was time-travelling, back two hundred, even two thousand years. Fragments of willow basketwork from Iron Age settlements at Glastonbury Lake Village and a Roman salt-making site on the River Huntspill were worked with the same weave as basketmakers use today. As I sat in dark attic rooms or chilly sheds, on the floor with today's basketmakers, drawing in my book, the whipping of the willows mixed with their reminiscences and I began to take my tape recorder with me. Then I learnt of the Oral History Archive at the Rural Life Museum and arranged to meet Ann Heeley and so our happy collaboration began. There are now more than thirty recordings of Somerset willow growers, basketmakers and others who are, or have been, involved with locally grown willow. The extracts contained in this book are fragments of these recordings.

The connection with charcoal was a revelation. I had no idea I was drawing with cooked Somerset willow, I'd been using it for years without realising. I was not just an observer after all, I was using the same willow too. The willow charcol drawing workshops in schools naturally followed on, often with basketmaking and willow sculpture, the children's charcol drawings vigorous and exuberant and an inspiration in themselves.

My scribbles in sketchbooks, charcoal drawings and paintings celebrate the people I have met. I am envious of their deep and ancient involvement with this haunting landscape and the willows they cultivate and craft, an involvement begun generations ago by their ancestors. It is their words that tell it from the inside.

I have travelled with my sketchbook and paints little more than ten miles from my back door, but I have visited other worlds. It's been a great journey.

SOMERSET RURAL LIFE MUSEUM ORAL HISTORY ARCHIVE

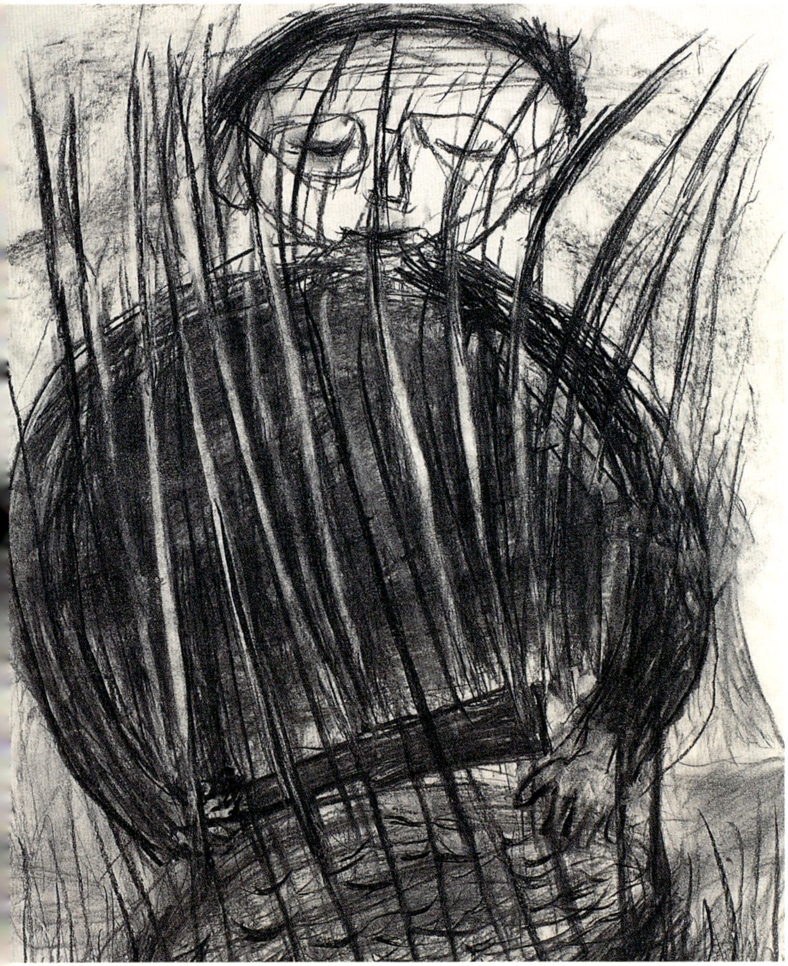

The Oral History Archive at the Somerset Rural Life Museum in Glastonbury began in a modest way in 1973 when it became apparent that, with the great technological advances that followed the Second World War, many of the old rural crafts and ways of life were rapidly disappearing. The work gathered momentum in 1979 when the Friends of the Museum, led by Ann Heeley, became involved, and, over the years since then, interviewing and recording has continued steadily. There are now more than three hundred and eighty recordings in the collection. Often these have been made as part of special projects. Most aspects of Somerset life, both in towns and villages, are reflected, and the traditional industries of farming, willow-growing and willow crafts, peat digging and cider-making, which still continue, are strongly represented, as are others that no longer exist, such as coal-mining. Nearly all the recordings are fully transcribed and a team of volunteers is currently working on an ambitious scheme to transfer the archive from their original recordings into digital form which will ensure its survival as a valuable source of reference for future generations.

The collection is freely available to all – students, researchers and the general public – on application to the Somerset Rural Life Museum on 01 458 831197. www.somerset.gov.uk/museums

Alf Brewer, basketmaker, Tim Rawlings, Aged 10

GROWERS, MAKERS AND OTHER PEOPLE FEATURED

Words quoted throughout the book are used with permission from the speakers and are edited extracts from recordings deposited in the Somerset Rural Life Museum, Glastonbury unless otherwise indicated. In brackets are: name of interviewer: AH (Ann Heeley), KL/JI (Kate Lynch and John Irving); date of interview; Somerset Rural Life Museum Oral Archive Ref.No. (SRLM OA). Full recordings and transcriptions of these, and other interviews, are available at the Somerset Rural Life Museum.

EDDIE BARNARD, Basketmaker, Middlezoy.
Born 1942, apprenticed at Gadsby's at 17, now self-employed. I made drawings of Eddie in February 02, warm golden light shafting in through his shed window, the willows looked on fire.
(Interview KL/JI 26th March 02, SRLM OA 367)

CHRIS BECK, Basketmaker, Curload.
Born 1963. Trained at Coates to make woven willow furniture by the legendary Albert Champion, in his 80's when he taught Chris. Now independent, Chris makes baskets, furniture and structures.
(Interview AH 8th May 02, SRLM OA 376)

DAVID BELLAMY
Author of 43 books and presenter of over 400 documentaries on natural history, ecology and the environment. President of Association of Master Thatchers, Conservation Foundation, Conservation Volunteers of Ireland, Wildlife Trusts, YHA and other organisations.

ALF BREWER, Basketmaker, Ashcott.
Born 1926. Alf was involved in the schools workshops and would like to pass on his skills in retirement (see his portrait by pupil Tim Rawlins on page 90). I made drawings of Alf at his workshop in Ashcott (Blackbird Baskets) just before it closed in February 01.
(Interview AH 17th July 01, SRLM OA 351)

ROB CHAMBERS, Millichamp and Hall,
Taunton Cricket Ground.
Born 1979. Cricket bat maker (English willow). When I was drawing at the workshop there was a constant stream of visitors, cyclist to collect a repair, mother for her boy's bat, friend in cricket whites and Nick Taylor knocking in a bat, "top of the range bats we do this in the price".
(Interview AH 23rd January 02, SRLM OA 366)

P.H. COATE & SON, Stoke St. Gregory,
Willow Growers, Artists' Charcoal, Baskets and willow products.
The willow charcoal connection inspired the school workshops (see Alf Brewer and Tim Rawlins). Coates run the Willows and Wetlands Visitor Centre, museum, shop and tea-room. I painted Mary Nash who works there.

SOPHIE COURTIOUR, Willow Sculptor, Rodney Stoke.
Born 1959. Created Leaping Roe Deer on Burnt House Farm, Marsh, with Stefan Jennings, commissioned by Blackdown Hills Rural Partnership. Works as sculptor and on willow projects in schools and with community groups. Studies Countryside Management part-time.

ANDY COX, Hurdlemaker/Riverbank Weaver, Curload.
Born 1966, works for English Hurdle on willow river bank conservation ("spiling") in the winter and hurdles and other outdoor structures in the summer.
(Interview AH 2nd August 2002, SRLM OA 381)

GEORGE DAVID, Willow Grower, Burrowbridge.
Born 1935. Mixed willow growing with small dairy herd and was hand-milking until five years ago. Manages own willow beds and boils for other growers. Reg Hector took me to see George boiling. Clouds of steam, frothy boiling water, sweet treacly wonderful smell of hot willows, I'd never seen or smelt anything like it. George's son, Jonathan, also works on the willows, for Coates.
(Interview AH 17th October 00, SRLM OA 347)

SERENA DE LA HEY, Willow Sculptor, Curload.
Best known for the Willow Man off the M5, Bridgwater, now a regional landmark. I climbed the scaffolding when Serena was weaving the man again after the burning of the first, she and Lucy near the top and me talking to myself to give myself courage as I climbed each vertical ladder, not looking down! I sat and made drawings four storeys up as Serena stuck willow sticks into the man's ribs as the wind buffetted, the plank floor wobbled, the odd hooter sounded hello from a pantechnicon thudding down the motorway.
(Interview AH 19th June 02, SRLM OA 379)

CHRIS DERHAM, Taunton.
Nephew of Stan Derham and works for Stan on the willows.

MAURICE DERHAM, Retired Willow Grower, Knapp, North Curry.
Born 1922. Was in the family willow business with his three brothers, Leslie, Reginald and Stan. I interviewed Maurice particularly for his memories of willow growing during the war, when there was a huge demand for willow baskets by the Air Ministry.
(Interview KL/JI 26th March 02, SRLM OA 368)

STAN DERHAM, Willow Grower, Knapp, North Curry.
Born 1934, father in farming and willow work. Stan and his three brothers, Leslie, Reginald and Maurice, all went into the family business. His brothers are now retired. I visited in March 01, the boiler steaming, he and nephew, Chris, in the stripping sheds. I was intoxicated, rich sweet smell of boiled willows, steaming wetness, hauling, pushing and pulling dark wet bundles, rich gleaming auburn redness of newly stripped wands. I wanted to convey something of the relentless physical work in that dark shed in my paintings.
(Interview AH 24 September 01, SRLM OA 356)

IVOR HANCOCK, Basketmaker, North Petherton.
Born 1934, trained with Mr. Carkett, North Petherton. Has been basketmaking all his life and independent for 50 years. His wife Joyce helps with the business. Both are involved with the Blackdown Hills Rural Partnership, Peat Moors Visitor Centre and the school workshops. Their son works for English Hurdle.
(Interview AH 23rd July 01, SRLM OA 352)

NIGEL HECTOR, English Hurdle, Curload, Stoke St. Gregory.
Born 1940, went into father's willow growing and farming business. Managing Director of English Hurdle, willow growing, hurdle making, outdoor structures, river bank conservation. The river bank "spiling" has a sculptural dimension, land art with a function.
(Interview AH 26th June 02, SRLM OA 380).

REG HECTOR, Willow Grower, North Curry.
Born 1923. Grandfather and father both in willow work. I first visited Reg in June 2000, Cliff Hembrow sorting withies on a long trailer in a shed . I wrote "time has stood much stiller here than where I've come from". In August I had tea in his kitchen and listened to his stories and in December on a steely grey day I found him and Mark cutting withies by hand with hooks on Wick Moor.
(Interviews AH 20th September 01 and KL/JI 24th January 02, SRLM OA 354).

CLIFFORD HEMBROW.
Born 1919. Grew up in North Curry, went to school with Reg Hector. Worked on the railways, now retired, still works part-time for Reg Hector, sorting and tying.
(Interview AH 13th April 01, Ref: SRLM OA 350)

ANDY HILL, Somerset Willow Company, Bridgwater.
Born 1969, Bridgwater. Sixteen years ago, he left school on the Friday, started basketmaking on the Monday, with his uncle, Aubrey Hill. I watched Andy carefully weaving an exquisite coffin, "I like making the coffins, they're getting more and more popular, and one-offs, too, anything unusual, trying to work out something you haven't done before, like the woven stag's head we made, or the horse-drawn carriage, even the filters for the ends of fireman's hoses."
(Quotation is from conversation with KL 12th November 02)

AUBREY HILL, Somerset Willow Company, Bridgwater.
Born Bridgwater 1935, father was a basketmaker, went into business together at North Petherton, then Bridgwater. Became the Somerset Willow Company, which trains and employs basketmakers and makes balloon baskets, furniture, coffins, other baskets and special commissions.
(Interview KL/JI 1st August, 01, SRLM OA 358).

DARRELL HILL, Somerset Willow Company, Bridgwater.
Born 1962. Trained and still works as basketmaker, now partner in the business with his wife, Heidi. His father, Aubrey, still works for the company, also sister Karen and cousin Andy. When I visited in November 02 they'd just completed a massive balloon basket to carry 16 people which was off to Africa on safaris.
(Quotation is from conversation with KL 12th November 02)

MIKE HUBBARD, Basketmaker, Chedzoy.
Born 1966. Mike's grandfather made baskets. Mike trained and worked with the Somerset Willow Company on leaving school. While I sketched he talked with passion about his work. "I avoid heating, it it's cold, you work faster to keep warm!". In today's over-centrally-heated indoor environments this sounds unbelievable, but, in general, basketmakers have little heating in their workshops, needing their willows damp and pliable. Now works as independent basketmaker.
(Interview AH 18th April 02, SRLM OA 371)

STEFAN JENNINGS, Willow Sculptor, Wellington.
Born 1962. Created Leaping Roe Deer on Burnt House Farm, Marsh with Sophie Courtiour, commissioned by Blackdown Hills Rural Partnership, also works on willow sculpture projects in schools and communities.

BRIAN LOCK, Willow Grower, Thorney
(E.M. and H.J. Lock).
Born 1950. Father and mother, Edith and Herbert Lock, both willow growers, Brian went into family willow business, joined by Brian White (brother-in-law) in 1970. I made drawings in May, their whitening season, newly stripped white willows gleaming in the sun.
(Interview AH 5th October 01, SRLM OA 359)

DOREEN LOVERIDGE, Retired basketmaker, Curload.
Born 1912. Recruited to make woven airborne panniers during the war. "It was better paid than a lot of other jobs, like farmworkers. We had better wages than they did... and I'd always been home before you see, just doing the housework and the garden". Stayed on basketmaking after the war.
(Interview KL/JI 3rd September 02, Ref: SRLM OA 387).

LESLIE MALE, Willow Grower, Stembridge.
Born 1927. Went into willow business with father, Earle Male. I met him cutting withies at Collins Bed, West Moor on a bleak January afternoon 2002 "snowfall forecast for tomorrow". Vernon drove the tractor, Les knelt on the moving platform gathering the cut withies as they fell. During our conversations Les recalled some 16mm film, shot in 1952 by his sister-in-law, Mona Chedzoy, showing his family growing and processing willows, which contains rare footage of the punting of willows along the rhines in flat-bottomed boats. Now on video, copies deposited with Somerset Rural Life Museum.
(Interview KL/JI 24th January 02, Ref: SRLM OA 369)

GUY MARTIN, Furniture Designer/Maker, Crewkerne.
Born 1946. Set up first practice in 1984 , Blackawton, South Devon. Taught at Parnham 1988-94. One-off designs to commission, also orders of repeatables, garden furniture, sculptures and fine wooden garden buildings. Moved to Greenham, near Crewkerne 1991.
(Quotation is from e-mail to KL 18th/19th November 02)

MICHAEL MUSGROVE, Willow Grower, Westonzoyland.
Born 1969. Went into family willow business with his father, Les. They have withy beds around Westonzoyland, Langport and Wick. Ellen, Michael's wife, helps with the business.
(Interview AH 5th October 01, SRLM OA 360)

LES MUSGROVE, Willow Grower, Westonzoyland.
Born 1928. Began cutting tree sticks for furniture with his father. "We used to do 'em white and I can remember him taking off with a pony, going into Bridgwater to sell them, then that died out and we started doing withies." Les still works in the business with his son, Michael.
(Interview AH 5th October 01, SRLM OA 360)

MARY NASH, Basketmaker, Stoke St. Gregory.
Born 1938, Trowbridge, Wiltshire, where father and grandparents worked for Loxleys, pigeon basketmakers. Father was Bill Bailey, started up on his own after 2nd World War as W.A.J. Bailey in Birmingham, then Stoke St. Gregory. Mary worked for her father. He died in 1969 and Coates, willow growers, bought the firm in 1977. Mary still works as a basketmaker for Coates.
(Interview KL/JI 3rd September 02, SRLM OA 386)

PETER NICHOLAS, Basketmaker, Stathe.
Born 1959. Trained as basketmaker in Stoke St. Gregory with Bill Bailey, then Gadsby's. Now independent. Pete was the first basketmaker I had ever seen working and the visual impact of the basketmaker seated on the floor, legs outstretched, the willow cage in front of him, willows soaring to the ceiling, the damp sweet smell, well, I was hooked!
(Interview KL/JI 6th June 01, SRLM OA 353)

STEPHEN PEARCE, Willow Grower, Stoke St. Gregory.
Father grew willows. Stephen returned to willow work after working in agricultural engineering. Sister, Helen Tyler, also has willow growing business.
(Quotation is from conversation with KL 13th November 02)

MARK PIPE. Born 1967.
Works for Reg Hector on the willows, like his father and grandfather before him.
(Interview AH 25th September 01, SRLM OA 357)

TIM RAWLINGS, Combwich.
Pupil at Otterhampton Primary School. Tim took part in the willow charcoal drawing workshop at the school and his lively charcoal portrait of Alf Brewer was exhibited at Coates Willow and Wetland Centre during Somerset Art Week 2002 with drawings from other schools.

ROGER ROGERS
Born 1949, grew up the fourth generation of peat diggers at Westhay. Ran Willows Peat Company (then Garden Centre) until 1994.
(Interview AH 24th March 01, SRLM OA 348 but quotation used is from conversation with KL 14th November 02)

BRENDAN SELLICK, Mudhorse Fisherman, Stolford.
Born 1934, Bridgwater. Father, grandfather and great-grandfather were fishermen at Stolford. Brendan is the last mudhorse fisherman, and his son, Adrien, is set to continue when Brendan retires. Traditionally fishermen throughout the country used willow for lobster pots, salmon traps, carrying and transporting fish. Brendan still uses his willow 'reap' to cool hot cooked shrimps. I gingerly walked across a quarter of a mile of dodgy mud to greet the mud horse returning from the middle of the estuary in September 01 and made drawings as Brendan cooked and cooled the shrimps back on land.
(Interview KL/JI 29/3/02, SRLM OA 384)

BRIAN WHITE, Willow Grower, Thorney (E.M. and H.J. Lock).
Born 1941. Works with Brian Lock, brother-in-law. Married into the willow growing business. His wife, Betty, helps with the business.
(Interviewed with Brian Lock, AH 5th October 01, SRLM OA 359)

HAROLD WRIGHT,
Spar Maker and Retired Master Thatcher, Compton Dundon.
Born 1920. Went into business with his father, master thatcher Billy Wright, when he was 14. Now retired from thatching, his sons and grandsons continue the business, but Harold still makes spars (in his greenhouse). "I like spar making, I don't know why, I always liked making spars – if we made 1,000 a day we could earn ten shillings a day, three shillings more than a farm labourer, I'll make 30,000 this winter if they can get the sticks." I made drawings late one December afternoon.
(Interview AH 4th April 02, SRLM OA 370)

ACKNOWLEDGEMENTS

I would like to thank all the willow growers, makers and others who have welcomed me into their sheds, their homes and their willow beds. It has been a huge privilege to meet them and this collection of pictures and words tells their story. I would also like to pay special tribute to Ann Heeley, a dedicated historian, who has collected the majority of the recordings, and John Irving, for his help recording and sound editing. This has been a happy collaboration and we would like to thank all those who have given interviews, spent time in conversation and allowed these edited extracts from their spoken words to be published in this book and used in the exhibition. We apologise to those people we have not been able to include.

Many people and organisations have helped with the project, exhibition, publication and school workshops. I am specially grateful to Tim Martin, Curator of The Phillips Gallery, Brewhouse, Taunton and to Sue Isherwood, Somerset County Council Arts Officer. Their help and encouragement throughout the project have been invaluable. I would also like to thank Wessex Water, South West Arts, Somerset County Council, The Lark Trust, and other benefactors, for their support. The project has received assistance from the Somerset Levels and Moors Partnership, Mendip, Sedgemoor, South Somerset and Taunton Deane District Councils and Littoral Projects Environment, also materials from St. Cuthberts Mill and P.H.Coate & Son.

I have enjoyed the working relationship with the Somerset County Museums Service, and would like to acknowledge the help of David Dawson and staff, in particular Mary Gryspeerdt at the Somerset Rural Life Museum, and Friends of the Rural Life Museum, especially Mary Vidal, Kath Cowles, Yvonne Penna and Theresa Levell Clarke, who transcribed the recorded interviews.

It has been a pleasure to link with galleries hosting the exhibition outside Somerset: The Platform Gallery, Clitheroe, Lancashire; Roots of Norfolk,The Norfolk Rural Life Museum, and Beaford Arts, Devon. I would like to acknowledge the generous contribution of the book designer, Catherine Phelps, and thank David Bellamy for writing the lively Foreword. This project has only been possible with the support and encouragement of my family and friends.

KATE LYNCH
January 2003

PAINTINGS AND DRAWINGS BY KATE LYNCH

ORAL HISTORY ARCHIVE

90 *Alf Brewer* willow charcoal drawing by Tim Rawlings (Otterhampton Primary School)

Front cover

Brian Lock in the pit with withies for stripping as white (page 25)

Inside front cover

Pete Nicholas, bordering down, willow charcoal drawing, 88x65cms

Inside back cover

George David patting the willows back, willow charcoal drawing, 93x65cms

Back cover

Eddie Barnard tapping the willows down tight, detail, (page 43)

Photography:

Leslie R. Warr FBIPP FMPA, David Wiltshire Photography and Nick Willcox-Brown.

KATE LYNCH BIOGRAPHY

Born 1949. BA Hons, History of Art, Essex; Art Teacher´s Diploma, Bristol University; Post Graduate Diploma, Fine Art, University of the West of England; Member Royal West of England Academy.

Solo Exhibitions:1993, 1996, 1998 Beaux Arts, Bath; 1998, 2000, Alpha House, Sherborne; 2001 Malthouse Gallery, East Lambrook; 2000, 2002 Somerset Art Weeks; 2003 'Willow' exhibition tour:*

Residencies & teaching: Artist-in-residence in schools and communities in the West Country; projects with Somerset Levels and Moors Partnership, Peat Moors Visitor Centre, National Children´s Homes, Kilve Court Education Centre, Jackdaws Educational Trust, Shute Farm Studio, Black Swan Art Centre.

*WILLOW EXHIBITION TOUR 2003:

Phillips Gallery, Brewhouse, Taunton 29 March – 10 May; Somerset Rural Life Museum 17 May – 29 June; Roots of Norfolk, Norfolk Rural Life Museum, near Dereham 5 July – 7 September; Platform Gallery, Clitheroe, Lancashire 19 September – 1 November; Beaford Arts (Village halls in North Devon)

Web: www.katelynch.co.uk

"I went all over the continent during the war but I didn't see anywhere better than home. Some say, why don't you give up the withies. I say, no, I'll give up when I'm ready to grow the daisies".

REG HECTOR
willow grower
North Curry